Jarl Alé de Basseville

My Duty

First volume: Reckoning

Éditions
DÉDICACES

First published by Editions Dedicaces in 2016

ISBN: 978-1-77076-596-2

This book was professionally typeset on Reedsy.
Find out more at reedsy.com

Contents

Foreword   i
Preface   iii

I   Family House

25 October 2012   3
26 October 2012   5
29 October 2012   7
30 October 2012   10
1 November 2012   13
2 November 2012   16
2 November 2012   19

II   Study and Suffering's Years

5 November 2012   25
6 November 2012   28
7 November 2012   31
10 November 2012   34
11 November 2012   37
12 November 2012   40
12 November 2012   43
14 November 2012   46
14 November 2012   49

III   Political Considerations

17 November 2012   55
18 November 2012   63
22 November 2012   66
23 November 2012   69
26 November 2012   72
2 December 2012   75
5 December 2012   78
8 December 2012   82
9 December 2012   85
13 December 2012   89
15 December 2012   92
15 December 2012   95
20 December 2012   99
21 December 2012   102
24 December 2012   105
24 December 2012   108

IV   Europe

30 December 2012   113
1 January 2013   116
9 January 2013   119
10 January 2013   122
17 January 2013   125
19 January 2013   128
20 January 2013   132
20 January 2013   134
26 January 2013   137

V   The Second World War and its Lies

2 February 2013	143
2 February 2013	146
9 February 2013	149
9 February 2013	152
17 February 2013	156

VI   Propaganda

24 February 2013	163
24 February 2013	166
3 March 2013	170

VII   Revolution

13 March 2013	177
20 March 2013	180

VIII   The Desire to Begin my Political Activity

21 March 2013	187
24 March 2013	191
4 April 2013	194

IX   People and Tradition

13 April 2013	201
13 April 2013	203
17 April 2013	206

X   The First Period of Development

29 April 2013	211
1 Mai 2013	214

1 Mai 2013	216
28 May 2013	219
12 June 2013	222
13 June 2013	225
12 October 2013	227
12 October 2013	230
21 October 2013	233
2 November 2013	236
2 November 2013	238
4 November 2013	241
8 November 2013	243
14 November 2013	249
15 November 2013	253
4 December 2013	255
15 November 2013	261
7 December 2013	264
9 December 2013	268
References	272

Foreword

Several people believe that the chivalry is only a fancy of the past, a soft memory for the nostalgic dreamers, but that's not the case. The chivalry of heart and spirit exists always today. It is an inheritance bequeathed by our ancestors who knew how to build the world in which we evolve, but whom we often strive to destroy for the simple lure of gain and of the power, or by pure individualistic egoism.

Jarl Alé de Basseville is a member of these knights of modern times, of those whose consciousness rises at the level of the people to extirpate the truths which will transform the current world. He is the one who denounces and who is not afraid of anything: *"this Europe rushes into the sewers of the carelessness and the conflict of state by hiding behind institutions created by the electoral little schemes"*. Proud descendant of king of England William the Conqueror, of the duke of Normandy Robert Courteheuse and of legendary Guilhelm de Gellone, Alé de Basseville immortalizes the tradition of the big destroyer of dragon, not only by denouncing the misdeeds of our governments, but by proposing solutions to the problems which invade us.

Born on July 8th, 1970 within an aristocratic family connected to the petroleum industry, he is trained trough the hardest jesuits boarding internships of France and Helvetia. The prince of this Normandy in Exile addresses in his speech to the tribes

Vikings, Celtic and Gothic who look for an explanation more deeper into on their traditions, identities and cultures. This government in exile claims in its way the fact of being the justifiable government, the purpose being to reconquer the power in his country to which it refers, to return to his own people : this is only his duty .

Jarl Alé of Basseville is also an artist and an accomplished photographer. During his career, he will have been next to the most renowned artists such as Andy Warhol, Lucchi Renato Chiesa, Jane Fonda, Tom Cruise, Valley Kilmer, Brad Pitt, Michael Jackson and Marilyn Manson. On July 31st, 2016, he created a real earthquake international politico-celebrity by agreeing to publish the photos which he had taken of Melania Trump nude in the New York Post, the most powerful American conservative republican newspapers.

Such as the Knights of the Round Table, Jarl Alé de Basseville pursues his road on this foreign earth in search of this Grail which will restore hope to the world. through in his words, he continues to shout out those who manage us in the only purpose to restore the balance in our world : *"the leader has to be the cement of the trust of his fellow countrymen and accept this duty which is his: bring the nation to the rank which she deserves"*.

Guy de BOUILLANNE
Regent of the Kingdom of Nova Francia
General manager of the Liberté-Nation Project

Preface

"To my grandson.
As nobles we don't have rights.
Only duties." - Albert de Basseville

So I decided to write and explain not only the goals of our movement, but also about its genesis.

In addition, I have the opportunity to set up my own formation. This could lead to the destruction of the legend about me invented by the press.

I am thus addressing the Viking, Celtic and Gothic tribes of our movement which seek a thorough explanation of our tradition, identities and culture.

It isn't unknown to me that it's the word much more than the books that won people: all great historic movements are due mainly to the speakers rather than writers, although ideologies were born there.

It's no less true that a doctrine can't save its unity and its consistency if it hasn't been fixed in writing once and for all.

Jarl Alé de BASSEVILLE

I

Family House

1

25 October 2012

I had the good fortune to be born in Bordeaux, city with a past so troublesome and so rich among the history of wars and markets linked to its harbor.

Europe must again become the great Celtic motherland, and this not pursuant to any economic reasons. No, absolutely not: even if the union, economically speaking, it's irrelevant or even harmful, it should take place anyway. The same blood belongs to the same Empire. The Viking people will not have right to political participation until it has brought all their sons together in a single State.

The plought will be then the sword, and the tears of war will produce the harvest and the bread for the tomorrow's future. And so my town appeared to me : as the symbol of a great task. It has other applicable chapters to our memory.

I lived in this town surrounded by my grandparents and by a powerful family, that was destroyed at the expense of fighting to conquer the Western Europe, which claimed to defend the capital rights from American ultra-liberalism. Only bulwark of communism in Eastern Europe and of its bad ghosts.

My parents were absent in view of this problem, but doesn't matter because that has strengthened my fighting spirit and my thirst for learning. My grandfather stood with me after himself has been deprived of everything because of this filthy war, that had spread throughout Europe. Not only by the crimes but also by its political involvement.

It would be rather difficult to say what life was, before my birth, of this grandfather, or father that he has been for me. But it would be easy to describe what he had become. He was the chairman of several societies and foundations and was called «Mr President».

In business, he was called «The Baron». But also, he loved to help the weakest who couldn't defend themselves. And he allowed some to call him «Berty» ; it was very funny to see these personalities passing constantly of «you» or «You» and «Mr . Berty».

This had a great impact on me in my youth and step-by-step, I learned all the tasks and charges to become a boss. I still remember the day I spoke about working in a nightclub - that he called « dance club » and for my grandmother was a place of debauchery and striptease girls - but it was my will to prove that money could be earned in the night that makes people dream, those who work in the morning and imagine that everything is possible in the night.

2

26 October 2012

If I have learned anything from my grandfather, he taught me what it means to be «noble» in the way that we only have duties but not rights. And that's this dear man, who after a huge past, never ceased to care about us and specially about me, this grandchild who answered after his question «What would you like to learn ?» «I want to know everything». And he wondered me again : «Yes, but the question is what ?» and me, saying «everything !!!!» until he would explain to me (looking at me with staring eyes) that was impossible to know everything. And seeing my disappointment, he bought me a leather and golden binding book.

The fact is that I've never thought about my future. I lived in a world of unreality, where I was the spoiled prince by an admired family. However, I don't remember why. I had my own thoughts and I felt within myself a determination to understand the politics and the economy, an all-consuming passion for geography when I was in front of the ship of my great grandfather, that went around the world several times, whose red tracks in the damaged card, under the glass of the house entrance, summarized this powerful Viking.

I was between the strength and the peace, like an eagle landed on a lake but that, at any time, it can pounce on a new prey. I loved singing, music, painting and I read with passion all the volumes of the First World War. I was passionate for the Vatican and all these decorum. There, I met Cardinal Guyot, who became a friend and I served as a choirboy for several years every Wednesday. I spent long afternoons with him. He used to tell me about the pre - Vatican II Church. I wanted to be Pope. Not a priest. No. Pope under the name Alexander VIII, one of my names and my rank the 8th.

But I lived in a confused time, where Europe was divided into two: a part called Western and a part called Eastern. One was liberty and capitalism, the other one, was prison and the Stalinist revolutionary communism post Khrushchev. In short, both worlds, or two blocks, were the battlefield of two monsters: Americans and Russians. And why did the take our land as a «war horse»? From that day forward, I thought that a country leader who would attack an other country leader, he just had to do it on a boxing ring !!! In the past, a noble could fight against another to take his land, and I perceived the stupidity of those people who lead us for their personal property.

My grandfather asked himself how I was going to live each day in fighting continually with my schoolmates. My family sent me to a boarding school and there, I finally understood what the sexuality was. And yes, it wasn't the time of boy's schools and the mixed were there for a long time. But it, my grandfather never imagined that, remaining on his views about old school...

3

29 October 2012

My grandfather's decisions were always conscious and weighed ; the sense was always there, which nothing and no one can back on it. He was a good and just man, with the Basseville's temper, it said among cousins. The Second World War made of him a different man and even if he had not lost the reason d'être, he still wanted to look across these difficult and trying times in a man's life. In these times, kids couldn't decide and he wanted to provide me everything that was forbidden in his youth and let me take my life and career into my own hands. But it's nevertheless certain that this man had to see something special in me, cause even he was tolerant , he would never has given me his trust as he did it.

As I said before, he was filled with a steady idea that life was a duty and it had to know to protect it.

I discovered the « not » and the desire to revolt against the orders, to name others and to seize this power so vulnerable by the force of a few men, I saw putsches to bring eastern countries, where -for years- the chaos and disaster of these unknown enemies reigned.

Also, I discovered two worlds : the public and the private. You were a civil and public servant or an entrepreneur, there was no doubt of that and May 1968 had given the power to Political sciences' children to be a little of both. I wanted to live my own life and I didn't see myself under the orders of a little chef wasting his time to encourage a crank that, being no longer oiled, had lost its usefulness. Yes, the world changes at all speed and it was enough to take the plane to realize it !

I learned so much in my family among my grandparents, aunts and uncles that I was bored at school. Simply because I had a photographic memory which allowed me to learn a poem in two minutes. History or any lesson to learn. It was for this reason that I loved Latin... I imagine that my enemies will make everything to find me against me all this youth and I didn't need them to say that I went from one school to another due to my behavior that wasn't undisciplined but simply dreamer. And yes, I was tired of hearing this poor professor skinning the Shakespearean language, so I preferred to imagine William among women and men featuring, then dive into the middle ages. I wanted, in my inner self, to fight. But why ? How ? At the same time, a visual arts teacher -who was also in fine arts-fell in awe of my drawing and paintings. I must to say that I was an enthusiast of Expressionist movement «Die Brücke» (The Bridge) that sums up itself the new state of grace in contemporary painting after the revolutions of «Dada». Painting permitted me to find myself and forget me. So I threw myself into this haven of madness that satisfied me. At least at that time, I thought it.

Art seemed the only way out in this life that I didn't understand and which only echoed the words «no future» in my head. Thinking that I could never see the year 2000 that seemed as a big mammoth tertiary. So, I had to «construct» me. Yes, but how ? As the life that revolved around me, it left me without a shadow of doubt where I expected something else to reconcile me with myself. From then, I decided to travel around the world and I wanted to do the maximum of experiences.

4

30 October 2012

My grandfather was proud that I could express myself through artistic creativity and he saw at me, I presume, the opportunity that he had not had to defy his dream because of this world war which had distracted everything and had put him in front of a terrible way to have a life with all that it may have as consequences. He decided to push and help me even if there were doubts about a path which may not be obvious. We talked about it but I did not see any future. That he feared the most was... that I dive into a frenzy uncontrolled of drugs. He asked aunt Caroline, who owned a film production company CSF, to take me for internships and to see if I was adapted to this environment which was not mine. Recommendations' aunt were extremely hard and I shouldn't disclose my identity to anyone. Thus I decided to use a nickname : Alé, which comes from Alesund, a norse Viking name and that gives the name Alexander, because France prohibited any name that was related to a saint ... Contradictory in a secular state! My aunt noted that I was not paid and that we would see what would happens. I was delighted and I became quickly - just a day later - second assistant director, becoming irreplaceable. And when anyone asked me about my name, I said him Conversano which only was understand by my aunt; and that's what happened. I arrived at the dining room at around 9:00 p.m., after the dinner, with the production, before my grandfather and my aunt who asked me loads of questions, surprised but delighted with what had happened. That night, I knew that I'd be paid for my work.

I was interested in anything. I wanted to know everything about everything, which annoyed my grandfather at the highest point. One day he spent a good time on explaining to me that we could not know everything. Anyway, I wanted to learn everything and I spent my time reading, which caused me problems for sharing with anyone what was in my life. Children irritated me, adults were often too silly for me and I was devoted anyway to ecumenical study. I remember one day, when I back home with a score of 10 out of 20 in physics, with a new teacher who scored with very special way. Beside the score, it appeared our rank, counting 4 classes so I was first. My mother did not believe me and insinuated that I had had to change or delete the rank so as not to be punish, while I had not any fear... But it was always stories with a mother who I never saw and who threw on me to shout or kiss me as if we were close when I couldn't bear her. My grandmother went to ask and it was explained her that this physics teacher was like that. He scored in that way because he was a professor at the university. I do not know if my grandmother was convinced, but that day, I realized that teaching was just ridiculous and I remarked it constantly at family lunches on Sunday at noon. Due to and because of these emotions and these tests, I became a little more myself in the revolt of learning and in the need for order of a lost world which was justified through the hardships of others. It was at this time when I loved politics and I wanted to look into it to the point of discovering the tools to seek out the truth.

I studied early 20th century to immersing the Industrial Revolution.

I became regionalist and I understood that Europe of the Regions which would eventually become my only political struggle until today. But I did not know it yet. It was extremely difficult to live knowing that we were separated between East and West because of two dictatorships. One of markets: the USA. The other, that of workers: the USSR. These countries echoed in my head as my enemies.

At least not in these countries themselves, but their leaders, whom I found as puppets on the television. I remember watching live assassination of Al Sadate. It was incredible, filmed live! That day, I realized for the first time that violence appeared to me as a wall in which I will cast me. Immediately I understood the claims and issues that would follow as the foundation of our civilization.

My desire to discover the Europe and, one day, to view it reconciled; if there wasn't an East and West, it would be that beyond geographic poles but that there would be a single Europe. One that has been so-called for centuries: the REICH. It had to revive in this continent our single culture, thanks to their tradition and identity that the world already envied us. One day, my way would be to revive this Europe of the Regions, which gathers around a single goal. Our people. The right of blood.

5

1 November 2012

It is obvious that in this Europe of the Regions, the rivalry of ancient cultures recalls that we were organized into castes at the time, until the fall of the Austro-Hungarian Empire that used these old ways life. Our calendar tells us that we are in the year 10194. This celebration is renewed from 21 to 25 December, our solstice, around a fir tree symbol of our faith in our father Odin. We are shared between 17,400 tribes and each of them was divided into 100 clans ; each clan was divided into 1,000 families or super-families.

Since the dawn of time the school is the beginning of relation-ships, arguments, envy and mockery but also it's the resonance of the policy and what parents may think. The call to fight is now for all these children of Celtic Viking Gothic tribes so that they know that they belong to a people elected by the Æsir.

"Know that you are a Vik Reich and you are part of the oldest people of mankind".

The soul of youth wants to hear a leader who represents all these qualities and leads at arms our tribes to regain our territories without any negotiation or compromise whichever.

In thousand forms, it will lead the fight to be free in the symbol advocated by William Wallace and with all weapons to defend themselves. It will refuse to sing foreign songs and it will exalt especially the glories of our people by referring to all the distinctive signs that some people wanted to use to deceive our world in the history of the 20th century. Youth will remember the great warriors and our fathers and grandfathers who fought for these achievements in the blood. It will wear the barred insignias of our people and our traditions to restore the shields banned by the false story told by liars and serving people who are just as our enemies forever. It is therefore in the small fairly reflection of great women. These warriors who have shaped our lives since the beginning of history, often with a better inspiration and better directed that a woman has been given with her milk that has flowed for the child that we have all been.

So I have the opportunity to take part in the struggle. I will shout out "Heil" to our symbols without fear as I have done since my childhood knowing that this is what I want. I want to see the dream of my family; in other words: the dream of our meeting, us, people cradle of humanity.

The imperial anthem will resound again and be proud braving ideas imported by our enemies to prevent from living. Our Europe must come together on behalf of those great parents died for this freedom and desire to be together, and our families are looking Walhalla. Clans of Europe regionalist hardly know anything of their race as their language, their tradition and their culture as a whole. I probably became a fanatic for some and for this only will to see my land empty of foreigners because we got there because those foreigners do not respect my ancestors and spit their hatred on the graves of our cemeteries.

I came to separate dynastic patriotism and regionalism race, with a clear inclination for this last.

The internal situation in the Habsburg Monarchy and the Bourbons only brought revolts between us because they handled political life in one way: divide and conquer.

The emblems of the royal and imperial past glory act for the wonderful prestige which belongs to every citizen since the fall of the conspirators who were Louis XVIII and Marie Antoinette Habsbrug.

On the day of the collapse of the Bourbons and the Habsburgs, the unanimous call, which reflects the deep sense slumbering in the heart of each one, explained by historical education, that the voices of the past speak softly of a new future and not make us forget that Spain still suffers and it is the same family who betrayed and plunged the Spanish in the black hole of a crisis lost while these same Bourbons strut in the luxury of government which was given by I don't know what committee and does not care about you, the ordinary citizen.

Today, the teaching of world history in primary and high schools is completely false and was written under the dictation of traitors. Teachers need to understand that the purpose of the teaching history is not to learn dates and facts.

History is there to remind us of what we do not want and what we do not want in our books. Teachers should to fight for the truth whatever it may be.

6

2 November 2012

A question comes to my head: What is my life if I am not doing what I must? Is my life to live in the poor survive and moving from school to a pre-accepted work by people who have decided for me, without a chance to extricate me from this life without color, without cravings, without vision to imagine anything other than smallness of being a cog for énarques and technocrats who decide at their desks about our lives and play with millions while eating caviar on our backs?

But this has always been the case and there was no difference in the last 100 years.

I have been fortunate to have in my family or even around people who rightly informed me and left my free will to the true history of our people and the complacency of this Diaspora that lead us by the nose and make us to go to the rod.

I remember the Cardinal Guyot who spoke to me and made me the reality of the memories of history, which for centuries had led the world without worrying about these so-called groups advocating their use today, but for me are problems, more or less long ladder, which will cause problems and require us to protect again and again. Well I say no! And like some people I say: help our people. It is of course unfortunate that Ethiopia or Haiti suffer after a few disasters that affect their people but it is not my problem No, today I want to give solutions to our society from youngest to oldest and design family as a source of life and common faith.

Yes Cardinal Guyot taught me but touched me deep in my heart and my soul to the point of tears feel pain at the corner of my eyes not being able to fight and gather what I'm trying today. He advised and made me react on problems of the past to illuminate the present because it is obvious that we were in the process of paying the bursts of the industrial revolution of the 19th century. For him, the honor was the feeling that was lost and gave way to a sense of shame. And why? I ask you.

It was a Cardinal, either. But a man who has kept telling me that any religion should lead our people and all temples had been based on political agreements. Secularism for him was the very symbol of the Vatican. It had been for centuries separated into two groups: religious and lay people who could control the Vatican because it is primarily a state with land, a constitution, diplomacy, bank... And not a religion made concepts and anyway based on human and not statements of cosmic forces ideas.

But how not to forget that these dynasties after Westphalia showed us the betrayal of the interests of our community for vile personal gains done today by foreign groups to empty us of our heritage.

What the Vatican reminds me every day is that these interest groups managed by the foul conspiracy of these people which we have welcomed as brothers and they have betrayed us for their own personal interests.

My love for my people's symbols is so strong that I can live and die for this faith. And what is it more beautiful than to live for a cause? Is it not the problem of the world and of this jealousy

17

perpetuated for centuries against us? Is it inconceivable that I nourish my cousin, my brother before a foreigner? That is what I am asking you. Is a crime to give to my people first? Once this last is satisfied and full, I give to others if I still have and only for this reason.

From North to South we have been asphyxiated by foreigners who not only fly but they betray our doctrines and devour the body of our people. The great houses make the game of successive governments in Europe for the sake of a few people who refuse to contribute to the welfare of our people under the banner of pay less taxes to meet their needs. The money's sacrifices of our people money for the last 20 years have been more extraordinary than acceptable.

My youth was made by crises and by an ultra-liberal capitalism at the expense of socio-political sources conducted by combatants in need of their state and not the people and even less of unity. I think, at least I am sure, that if we want to fight politically, this feeling has absolutely no relationship with money and power but rather for reconciliation and the glorious outcome of our people.

Through my writings and this book I will explain and give details of the truth of European companies and their lies. But also the inability of governments to respond since they are not even able to know how to work their own social security and that are only recipients who allow themselves to judge those who do not have the means to these policies which are one and the same way to.

7

2 November 2012

The salvation of our people has the greatness of our history and its historical representation.

Should I ask my supporters to demonstrate dice this fidelity to our dynasty and to wear the colors loud and clear. Our dignity comes from our sense of regional experience and share the research of policy absolute. How to love this Europe today when everything has been removed and I don't feel be at my home but at the home of these foreigners who have condemned my empire to be theirs.

These foreigners will never understand that they are guests and I'll have to call them to order in a violent manner if they do not want to hear the gentle way.

But if you came to our home it is to earn money! To find something that you could not have in your country! Or because you were in danger due to your commitments! So why now you take the wrong roads imagining that this blood land belongs to you? When you've never done that steal us to buy houses or other objects for your own families in your country. You only steal our barns wheat and pollute us with your racist, xenophobic and backward.

You have created my soul the hatred against you because you came to disturb my customs imposing yours as if I had to accept them as if you accept mine in your own country. For me honor, courage and love are the only symbols of freedom that I support and I know that these words end up in gags in your consciousness.

At school I was prepared to fight this universal history that you want to serve me in the guise of a democracy and you are unable to give me the meaning. The policy of the private Christian school taught me about the revolutionary plans of these principles which are ours and represent our ongoing battle.

The result of my childhood was the change and controversy in the absolute conviction to experience the enthusiasm of these excesses pushing a teenager in purple rivers' worship of a people advocated by a grandfather people still amazed by a time past in the 30's and who dreamed of a new order.

Have I gone through the puberty? I'm not sure; my uncle repeatedly told me that even if I had ahead of others, thanks to family education, I always had to be the first and I never rest. So I felt lost and alone, taking refuge in the logic of the books. I had to search on myself how I can live in this world that I found more ugly by these lies and worse! This nonsense.

I became painter to escape from the truth of life and by convincing me that I could live my difference in the 1 percent without doubt that one day groups would do anything to hurt me and take up arms against who destroys the unbreakable.

I know that I was protected by grandparents who wanted to hide me the truth, the life but who loved me so much that they have sacrificed everything for this little-grandson who was one continuous question mark, always asking and who lived in a world amazed.

I advanced in this large and immense alley of chestnuts, imagining me I do not know what about life and thinking that everything resembled that I knew with the unconcern of a child.

Yes, I was there alone and surrounded by thousand people to go to a place that I would find at the heart of my travels and that would not stop until the day I decide to live my life and not be afraid of my self.

II

Study and Suffering's Years

8

5 November 2012

For me, adolescence was not a time of joy and hope but a burning desire to kill myself because I gave up living in a world that seemed to me without any expectations. I must say that we were in 1985 and at that time, the future of political correctness was rather invisible or nonexistent. I traveled and spent my time in New York. A city that seemed to me at the time, welcoming and so different! I must say that this city has nothing to do with the one you know today ... To tell you the security there was permanent. Everyone knew one another and after two days, even it was known what you drank in the morning or night. Brief. It was a heavenly city where we felt like we were away from everything because no laptop, no emails, only phones in the streets with their prepaid cards. But what freedom! I floated in an artistic environment where all have become known. But also most of them are dead ... Diseases such as AIDS, but overdoses too.

How lucky to live between workshops and museums! I tried the Polaroid film camera and I learned the room and I loved that which appeared upside down and which proved so rapidly picture. The same meaning of the painting. I bounced on to movies, from 8 to 16 mm projection on painting the walls and the ultimate test of carving stone or marble ... Everything was beautiful. Everything was possible. We lived without the word "money" and the policies of any kind did not exist. Only art and creation were at the heart of the debate, sometimes so animated that some came to the hands ... At this point slug it out. Of course, we were of drunk alcohol, drugs and happiness. Our song was that of La Bohème by Charles Aznavour that resonated with us as the only way to the dictatorship of art, so identified in the surrealist manifesto of André Breton. Our teacher was peaceful but suffered from chronic diseases certainly because of the attack which he was the principal actor. But he never had one word louder than the other and everything reminded him that the human soul has two functions: creating and directing. When we were talking about us, we were the "1 percent" and the rest were only to respond to marketing inventions that we experienced at full speed to see how far the human being could go and how he became the slave of a company that blew him the idea of being free. Free as a pig in a pen that can do only one thing: eat her shit because we had decided for them.

The only feeling that I had about myself was pride. When I hear people say that they went to a night club and they succeeded have to return after waiting, I've never asked the question and I arrived as if I was Apollo which everyone expected, making the wind at physio transsexual and all the wildlife that ran these places, always as if they were slaves and that I understand better than anyone the world. I must say that if my art master pushed me such an action, Aunt Caroline continued to encourage me on this voice seeing in me this potential public relations and network. Word that was not used at the time. But that communication was for cash!

I felt alone and weak. I understood that my duty now is to

find me in a moment of inner suffering until I finally would find
the true way to share my state of mind, if there is a way to live
however...

I then wrote a few words providing a collection of poems that
was stolen by a girl which I won't mention the name yet but I
will reveal it soon:

Le désespoir est un espoir/ Despair is a hope
D'un lendemain trahi / On a tomorrow betrayed
Pour lequel on vit / Which we live for
Dans un délire inédit/ In an unprecedented frenzy.

9

6 November 2012

What happens in the mind of a child? Why so much hatred? All these questions, their why... and I'm looking for answers.

It is obvious that the first thing that comes to mind is revenge and how to make it. But also why they are so angry with me. Is that I was not wrong way? And anyway, what my dream was? Me strutting alongside artists of lousy and poorly fagoted or other wearing pajamas for the air of something, and who under the reverse power, hid patients desperate for fame.

I wanted to discover this goal and call became more and more consistent. I never really realized life until I found myself in Milan, Italy, to live an artistic life that will have on me a special need. I lived next to Florence, Rome and Lake Varese. This is where I discovered Mussolini and complexity of the industry and Italian politics. I approached the great of this world between Gianni Versace, the scholar, and Raoul Gardini, the guardian of the Golden Gate. But with all that I would meet some of my unknown story hidden in Naples and Bari. The history of this family Basseville of Normandy changed forever the story that I had made during those interminable dinners on Sunday.

My pride was returned. It is not that it had really disappeared, but has it taught me to have one? Perhaps, in a pinch, when I was in scouts ... It is true, through boxer my mates and hurt them to the point that I took pleasure and I realized how much it has défoulait me and positioned before the chiefs who didn't see me as a child despite my age. Yes, I went to Naples and I felt one look at me as if all the Napolitan knew who I was; so did I look like my ancestors -or was it some sign?

At the time, I dressed all vinyl and leather. I had long hair long or mid, pointed boots with metal tips to hurt (laughs). I saw my name everywhere and this ancestor Robert Basseville who had cornered the city to himself but who was ...... What was he for me, for my future? Returning to Milan, I asked questions to my friends, glad to know who I was, made me discover the secret lodges of power and societies that populate the money and wealths called conveniences among others. I "sailed" without realizing it in a environment so implausible that any human being would probably find this suspect, but that for me was totally natural.

I wanted to be hard but I was a high person in Catholic schools. Not only the teaching of Saint John Baptist de la Salle, who helped his upcoming but a hatred grew within me. It took when an idiot two years my elder, turns on me one day to annoy me with a pen for me to and to understand that I was changing when I jumped on him like a vampire thirst for blood.

I was a child too pampered, adored by grandparents who raised me like a prince. A child who was thrown despite himself into the world of this great misery and the human stupidity which introduced him to those for which he was later to fight without stopping.[1]

---

[1] It was at this time that my eyes were opened to two dangers that I barely knew and whose name I have no suspected the terrible significance for the existence of the Viking people, Muslims and communists.

These happy festive places were, unfortunately for me, a living memory of the saddest period of my life, between drugs and decadence as if we were lost and the only watchword was "no future".

What means to be a man but to become an adult? Is it not in the experiences and excess accompanied by the essence where one becomes that which one must be? Are there not a way that resonates between everything and everything in the collective unconscious and meets the "why" so-called lost in the troubles of living space almost people.

I had to plan ahead and yet my unfailing disregard for life would lead me to the care of the influence of the forces of good and evil in this world eager to tap in me that would forever remain buried like the lamp of geniuses ever woken up in the sandstone live eternal war. Yes, I prayed Odin Wottan it gives me the strength to fight and become what life was to make me: a knight.

10

7 November 2012

Then, I asked me the question: will this genius in me choke fears of this intoxicating and disproportionate youth at the point to take of it the misery of a human existence translated by the doctrines of Kant ? Was my life really the same one as the others? I was not unaware of the life and his physical or mental sufferings which were thrown on me like an uncontrolled wave, a tidal wave. What wanted to say "social"; in a world of unconcern and contempt of art?

My life was that of a bourgeois. A citizen who had been a terrible child called "bad boy". I could, it is true, beat me to school or get drunk very young throwing me on who would like. Finally to finish with myself. In this case I did not accept. And why so much hatred towards my person? If it is because of these people who reproached me these stories of these wars that I had not lived. I had to hide myself because of to have been a German Viking believer in the Reich.

I had doubts and I tried to understand the duties which my grandfather indicated to me.The chance did not lie only in studies but also emanated from this force called the intelligence, which was not close to all. Our duty was to share it for these working classes which had not had the same chance as me.

In fact, the reason for all and all political demands, whether from the east or from the west, were work against the regime of poverty former. They were not so proud to be a must for example be cleaner called "surface technician" to bring him a reason to be when the only reason is the execution of a job well done. Since when a street sweeper was not allowed to read books and novels to escape? Not in its natural person but in the philosophical idea of the idea of being the Man of 1789.

Nevertheless, social crises and economic crises should give this energy to create a spirit of a single voice to shout other people without tradition that identity which sets up a unique culture that the world envies us so much. We lived under the skies of a sky deprived of colors as I said little time ago in a poem which I will allow myself to quote once more.

Rien de vu dans un ciel dépourvu/ Nothing of seen in a deprived sky
De couleurs/ Colors
Qui croit dans un espoir incertain/ Who believes in a dubious hope
Que l'aube d'un jour/ That the one day old paddle
Arrive là où le soleil se couche/ Arrive where the sun lies down

These words of my mouth which still reflect this collection of poems but which covers the violence of a child now in charge of stories by a glorious and victorious past of all those which wanted to destroy it. I won against the only person that has a weapon to defeat the point where the impossible was made against them. Since the accountant of Al Capone, as my lawyer had specified me, nobody had success to ridicule them... Finally, especially now in this century, if my grandfather had been able to see this, undoubtedly he could not have believed in it.

I summarize: so I had to be destroyed as many members of the family who ruled thereafter over Europe to understand the pain and let me by myself without any help whatever they are.

I had woke up and I forget the mercy and compassion of any kind. Otherwise, I could not manage a people, a land with all the pride that entails.

So this world has brought misery and insecurity, I was able to overtake him having seen the worst and most importantly remembering every moment of those moments when I could not decide my free will and being forced as I had been in as a boarder. But really, there is not a prisoner of the impossible, or as a philosopher said: *"Is it not to be a prisoner of the useless that makes us be broken and helpless"*.

If the court of the Empire attracted the human. He who waits with all his intelligence the right to dominate the state and centralize systems until end comes, it even has led these families Bourbon and Hapsburg to imagine as great Odin Wotttan.

It was necessary to give birth to this new centralization of the Empire a land of all tribes in the context of a shared freedom as it was shouted by the Gothic fighters as a whole.

11

10 November 2012

Paris was the political centre of Europe. Even if Brussels and Strasbourg played the game to be important in empty Europe of constitution. All these old last republics marked as of monarchies which changed only figure. But the political families benefited from all the advantages so much so that 5th was only the unquestionable copy of 4th, itself recovery it third. For the single system of the profits of a single group always with the power called technocrats.

How to explain the systems and the changes of those when it is known that all these people like the soldiers, the civil servant and the artists of intelligentsia do nothing but suffer from the decisions of some members who do not even know the price of the bread. I see only thousands of increasingly many unemployed before the institutions and in their heart the tears of despair. The suffering not to more be to trust to be European and to want to fight: yes my friends. Do not ask what your country can do for you. But ask yourself what you can do for your country. What will happen to all this middle class is losing their job and why these crises repetition.

Are you really sure that a German professor is able to solve the problems of the crisis, to find work or to save businesses.

Even better: do you think the President can meet your needs without knowing what it means to live simply with the minimum wage while he, with his wife, followed the path of the ENA and therefore decided not to not understand your worries. Yes! They do not or no longer know what it's like to struggle with bills and administrations. All these institutions are not able to answer your waiting because they do not have idea of what are your waiting and does not know what wants to say to work. On the other hand, they are the first has to be glorified and to go in the name of other parties which are only their friends of heart. That which we need, it is of a radical change.

This Europe is engulfed in the sewers of neglect and conflict state hiding behind the institutions created by electoral schemes. Do you know really which is your deputy? Do you know who does what for you and your interests, not his reelection. Social issues can not be made on a European level but in each case, with a definition of the order and will of each to act as consequences.

Anyone who does not see reduced in misery, can not understand what humans can endure and certainly not the politicians who hide in a soft and attractive home.

This Europe is engulfed in the sewers of neglect and conflict state hiding behind the institutions created by electoral schemes. Do you know really which is your deputy? Do you know who does what for you and your interests, not his reelection. Social issues can not be made on a European level but in each case, with a definition of the order and will of each to act as consequences.

Anyone who does not see reduced in misery, can not understand what humans can endure and certainly not the politicians who hide in a soft and attractive home.

35

What I can tell you is that I am against this false sentimentality organized by the ministerial groups to touch you and make you become lambs. I'm against superficial chatter and I will fight anyway all these vile ways to make you believe that there is a possibility of finding a job. I will also send you through my writings demonstrate the possibility of a job for everyone.

I want to share with you the fear of the majority of opportunities and their difference. Most harmful to you is the same managed laughing social misery by filling the pockets of indirect taxes such as VAT.

12

11 November 2012

Thank you to those snobs women who speak with an arrogant tone and live in mansions in the 16th arrondissement with an arrogant and condescending untied of any tact. Themselves who play the women of the people by creating foundations to enrich themselves on the backs of taxpayers. These people are mistaken if they believe that I won't do anything to prevent and throw in prison the day when we'll arrive into the power. Yes, they will pay for their crimes and conspiracies they are now at the helm with the consent of their husbands. The people must come to power and give it to the people who will fight for the identity of this one so much so that the whole world will be obliged to be turned over on to answer us and answer us. Do not be surprised ladies and gentlemen deputies, the people does not give you any success. How can we assign you a success when the only thing that you represent is indeed a meeting that would have sent Robespierre to the guillotine for breaches of the rights of the people, agreeing well against revolutionary privileges.

How to claim any recognition when one try to develop a social activity for the good of others? Isn't this a means of finding still an escape ahead? I'm not here to give favors to anyone, but to provide work for every European who represents the traditions of our people. I studied social issue at length through and I see only one possibility. That create social order that does not exist because of political technocrats drifts past 20 years. Should I become a soldier of an army without a trade and not an army of a country proud to bear arms against the enemy? Isn't this thus all these people who directed our companies which destroyed our world?

We were the guinea-pigs without a political order and without morals. But, even worse, no purpose and no state vision.

We were the guinea pigs without a political order and without morals. But, even worse, no purpose and no state vision.

It is extremely laughable to see that I grew up as a child who believed in values but that those were taught by my parents and my teaching In any case by the State, which is more than non-existent and represents for me the largest horde of impostors and robbers who leave only the remarks non-cohesive with the truth of a dependence at the 21st century.

What should I say about our society today living through Facebook and Twitter, Is this the answer that our people expect? I do not think so. They are only people who live through Internet and who are not able to go down in the street to express.

The situation of Europe must change and we have to stop the crippling considerations of duty and blood.

I will fight for Europe with ruthless purpose to rebuild its lives in a new world and reconquer our only fatherland. I understood that only work is honorable. I do not say "was" but "is" and I must say that to fight to keep it is a right which consolidates my idea that human beings are born to live together in this European mother.

This insecurity of our daily life is made of fears and anxieties also created by some media ready for anything to make us fall into total chaos. But will know that it is not new and that the press never ceased pushing the Men with the fight baited against the order.

Yes the order is hated by the press, the media and politicians because the order is the only way out of the crisis and consider the 21st century.

The 30's and the war of oil in the 70s it had announced the return of crises and problems of a society based on money and not on the value and respect of the human.

It is possible that it works in the U.S. or Asia. But in contrast to others, our Europe is built on 35,000 years, in a land where we lived and survived always finding different ways to fight and pass the caps and pass the courses whatever they are.

Immigration was understanding until the internet happens because there aren't more opportunities for all these people to come here, to make money or find a job. There is evidence that China has managed to make its companies an economic structure surging without having to travel, selling by mail. Companies such as Ebay prove every day that one can buy and sell without moving of course. Understand the usefulness of communications such as Skype in order to share information online.

It will be necessary that I explain you how the media and the policies make use of immigration as a source of problems when a solution exists.

13

12 November 2012

What wants to say these years of studies and suffering when I speak about economies and policies? Is this not a way for me to get into the heart of the matter? This is not what is expected of me to talk about the unemployment while I did not even know that unemployment meant as an artist because it is a job that requires waking up all days to get a new contract. Yes so I did not think to put me out of work and make thousands of statements to suck the ecu of the nation Yes, I saw misery. Even as I would never have imagined to see or to know because it is true that my grandparents took me to live in a world where the villain does not exist, as a friend specified it one day like Siddhârta Yes, indeed and surely to live and discover what there is outside the world that I did not know these famished.

To sell and pawn what one has, namely anything or almost nothing, was for me once again something about which I hardly worried at the time and which I discovered in my uncle. The fact of having or not a housing it is true in the 80 was not a worry. But I saw this gangrene to threaten a world which I thought untouchable. Yes, when we spoke of the poor it was always the images of Ethiopia and Somalia that we came out to us as and history give us a bad conscience for the newspaper of 20:00 with a journalist who had the looked so sad that it seemed he had lost his entire family. It was not presenter he should have done but reality TV actor. Yes but at the time John de Mol did not exist on the small screen at least.

All of a sudden came an evil which, according to my grand-mother, disappeared after the second World War. It is true that in the reconstruction of a world and the development of Western Europe, we had forgotten the basic principles. Yes, war, my God it's good for the economy! Especially that it will cost how many lives? 50, 75 or even 100 million? Surely more... One found these problems which re-appeared: employment, unemployment and poverty. I acknowledge that I did not understand. I worked enormously for my part because my grandfather had inculcated to me work not like labor but like source of joy, peace and interior achievement.

I did not continue absolutely the profits but a desire for living and not for surviving. Without imagining that the state should assist the creation of work. To tell truth, at the time I saw the state as a financial abyss. Coverage of the western world who told us a thousand and one things about the world and its famous drifts. At the time in Italy, this is where I discovered the political parties without any conviction. As the party of the Christian Democrats ... That good marketing slogan of communication that does not mean anything. But, this was a return to the ideas unfounded as the gathering of the people of the republic. What does that mean? Nothing In any case, not more than banal publicity of a yoghurt.

Right. After all, what were the values of the state? Was there at least? Certainly not! And not with ridiculous characters like Giscard who strutted to go drink coffee with street sweepers that we would come out of a crisis that had been started on the day of the industrial revolution and the advent black gold. No, we were in the threat of political correctness of the right-wing groups who kept talking impostors as de Gaulle, as if it was a living God, a new Buddha can be. The funny thing is that it was clear their name with each new election.

Bread has been the concern of the French revolution. The work has been the concern of this revolt rumbles for so long. Here the human wanted to work and wanted a social security because you would have to believe it was … What? Social law? Yes, perfectly. So the concept of modern man who must spend to live. When we say live is to live well, of course.

I remember this exhibition in Milan where an artist had decided to expose boxes full of shit and sell dear. Well everything has been sold to museums. Do not laugh it is with our money, that of the taxes.

14

12 November 2012

Housing is now a real problem because it is true that you are asked as many documents as you can make the day you want to become a tenant. But when I was 18 years old one rented in two minutes and one changed apartment almost every month because of being well to change. Nobody wants to live in one place too long. Of course, the rent was paid but it is true that at the time there was so much work that it was easy to gain it was necessary to pay the daily newspaper.

Today, I am ashamed when I see these these over-populated residences that have been destroyed by these foreign units. Even those who came to steal our daily bread and destroyed the very symbol of our currency: to fight for our country.

To pass from the private schools or known as private because they do not receive the State aid and correspond to a model which is not given has everyone. We belonged to the elite, that one even which was to direct Western Europe. That one even which was friendly of the United States of America. That one even which could not move only because too naive and too apprehensive.

When I use the word "we" is a "we" a bit special because I grew up in a "we." "Us" selfish and egocentric where we provide it and the rights.

The rights to do what we wanted with the blessing of the member countries of NATO. In short, we had none. And fear of war breaking out at any time between USA and Russia while living on another planet that we were not part. Our only duty was to watch the space through their images and battles. The great movie Sunday night was a great Hollywood movie where everything was to the glory of country stars. Probably not the image of what we believe, we did a certain Lafayette, General in addition, that would have made the American revolution.

Live with this wall is ... But what is happening and why? I did not understand this story and why this communist one day I spew Marxist ideology as it was a ploy petty bourgeois as was also the famous May 68. Result of a small group of lighted who wanted to take the power of their own fathers denouncing the cartoons of fascist past that they had not known . That without to move their bottom of dirty small middle-class man eating the bread of is saying reactionaries.

Yes, the sad spectacle lies. Here what I started to foresee. How was I going to make my way in this world of cruelty and in which I suffered but I could not speak? I discovered several movements at the beginning which made me enormously more. Like punk because he hated the hippies of the 70's of course I did not know. I hated the priests connected with their guitar and singing songs a smile idiot half Jesus, half revolutionists Bolsheviks. No. Me I preferred the priests who sang the Latin mass and who had refused the Vatican II to follow Monsignor Lefebvre.

The tables opposite me were made already see despair and the sad results which the future economic decisions of Europe would have. This one even which will be believed free in the point to make in a democratic idea a meeting to create an economic exchange that, still today, remains an utopia.

Yes, shared between punk and Latin church, I felt alone in front of a wall without answers. So I decided that I would experience in my life until I find the way to accomplish my desire. I became so special class in that they thought I was antisocial. What mattered more to me because I found the teachers and ridiculous anyway slaves of a lost society. Yet it was at the same time that I discovered the world of girls and all that was involved and why we should be with them.

If I were a poet, so I would say that adolescence is extremely difficult and there are no solutions if the New Order is not there to bring these solutions to feel as supported. I had the advantage of having had a grandfather but also being surrounded by family and many artists and intellectuals who have accompanied this life that was given me this desire to independence has allowed me to live in a pseudo carelessness. Probably gave me the desire to travel to feel free.

Yes. Freedom and nature are the bases of being a Viking. From where these references has this natural mother source of the freedom shouted until today in the wars of roses. Nature is not concerned as to the conservation of being and the growth of its offspring. It is the same in life and death according to Asgaard. There is little reason to artificially enhance the bad sides of this – better to impossible – but to prepare healthier ways to the future development of man by taking in its infancy.

15

14 November 2012

I am often asked during my adolescence if I could be proud of my nation. Viking nation of course. What are the feelings that I would make to increase this heritage that has made me a different being.

We belong to the people Viking, these privileged, beautiful, large and robust people! The whole world saw it so much it is strong and intoxicating. At all times, the people and the men tried to imitate us, taking or inventing values gothico- celtico viks but very often turning over them in values very far from ours, which often causes terrible confusions.

How individuals and groups can submit commercial logos, which for the most part, are made emblems for us represent the values of battles, families and clans who fought for the empire: the Reich.

Is it not once more the way for some lobbyists who try to find out what our people and destroy our nation forever? Well, I tell you. It will be impossible as long as I live. How many realize that their quite natural pride of belonging to a privileged people? Are connected by an infinite number of links to everything that made their country so great in all areas of art and spirit? The pride of being Viking comes from the knowledge of these ancestral ashes. The people is not a utensil that comes and goes. No, it is the people elected. Whoever did dream to the point of copying, love until idolatry. Fills a symbolic hatred terrace links those with nothing or very little.

It was difficult for me to understand and accept my difference. Thousands of people are jealous of me because they simply do not know where they come from. I even panicked and hid myself from my Viking ancestry. They had a dangerous character after the last historical events, featuring the victorious fighters of the Second World War. When I say they were victorious for me. But of course, not to impostors who arrived there to place as they say. We often see it today. They are called the ''faillots'' besides in progress... Or bootlicker, as you prefer.

Some will consider me as chauvinistic and I tell them that I exalts the greatness of the regions of Europe. In all fields of culture to civilization. I realize and I want to share with all the youth who would experience an evil being that education Reich give him as he was giving me the objectivity and the reality of the world. But with one difference: I'll be there to tell them and relieve them in their doubts. We must fight for the greatness of our great nation. We must live for the nation. There is no use of living for himself. This is a made concept of lies. For my friends, our land and a land of blood. If I take again the concept of the Gallic village, you would understand it quite simply. We have grows with image of Astérix and Obélix of the cartoons of the women sublimes, large goddesses Vikings and I refuse any other tradition on my ground. Because my friends, our ground is a ground of blood. Any being which would not be blood of the 17400 tribes Vikings will not be entitled to this heritage and will be able to remain if it combines no hatreds against our clans there.

At the school and in adolescence, I would have seen only rats running on the ship and which will have done everything to use our images and to destroy the memory as of our famous ancestors. Yes my friends. You see, we talk about destruction when I want to call you to rebuild our nation. We must unite together and bring concepts to the faith of our image and even united symbol on politics.

With which age a child does learn on his origins and becomes aware of this memory and what the fact represents of being part of chosen people? And what do I have to tell him? That we are in the same problems as the Thirties which carried out our people to take again the reindeer's but to trust groups which knew to create investment fund called hedge funds and which developed the crises since 1970. Then I told you. Let us not trust any more these policies that we must stop and put in prison. We will see then how they manage with their states of hearts.

16

14 November 2012

The conflict parent-child can sometimes be used for the nation because it can lead it must emerge- to a harmony together for the good of our people. To have traveled in search of essence led me to understand the world and what Natural Mother offered to me since I was born. It is true that these years in Milan were extraordinary because I met clothes designers of reputations, lawyers close to the dignitaries of Italy. Moreover, this country did not exist and has always been a set of regions called principalities, duchies, counties or baronies and, of course, the Papal States. I approached people I can quote but this is not important. I do not want to fall into a "gossip" policy. To say what? Did I meet the son or daughter of this or that political person who was so important during certain years of war? I must I tell you the truth. And what I have lived, if I write today is to give you the system that allows me to make you understand that I will not ever want to find myself in this situation in which I am I fight tooth and nail to the end to finishwith what is happening in our people as we are advocating single value.

This return in Italy asked me to focus on the state and what it meant symbol of morality and the nation in the present society in the heart of the men of faith. Often asked me why I had my long hair. Then I could see once again the lack of culture of our nations. And yes, we did not have the right to cut our hair at least we could during the summer solstice and Christmas Day – New Year's Viking 21 to 25 December. We need sacred and hair are the source of the sacred in both directions, as I can state it. If you had left me like a child who may be at fifteen, said a critic of authority, I would not have learned about the mud and the rubbish which are the exclusion of anything that could uproot me.

I grew up in a world where we did not allow much of what we tolerate today. Policies show themselves to us as normal. But if policies go wrong, what should I tell the media that are more than ever null and which are pseudo politically correct? Why I actually do not like politically correct? Because they have no convictions and allow themselves to give you everything is going good intentions. I learned a lot with people who are not afraid to fight in the sense of becoming and being. I do not want to talk about me and my life because this is not the goal and I do not find any interest. Anyway, it would be anti myself, just to congratulate me. I lai fact I did. If some journalists want to write crap on me, I do not give them the means. I am the man who has been with hundreds of young and beautiful women … Oh my God! And yes, I'm not rotating as some of these young people from these famous cities which have been so scared … Oh my God! What I'm afraid! It's really anything … They set fire to plastic bins … Oh this is amazing! How horrible! …

All I've done is my business and experience have given me the power to discover and understand who I am facing the beings who have only one desire: to destroy what we are because they are all just jealous of us and our traditions.

1111

11111111111111111111

I do not want any with my detractors. Quite to the contrary. They made me become a man and now I know what I want and where I go. Yes. My grandfather was right. It is necessary to live and learn while protecting that we have of more beautiful: nature.

III

Political Considerations

17

17 November 2012

Now I know why we can not get into active politics before age 40. One can hardly live in harmony with people if we do not face the impossible, the unspeakable, intolerable. The aim of the policy is not to be part of a platform, a right or left political system that no longer looks at a set of people who want the security of a chair lounges. Consider the problems of politics and build together the Viking nations party, for the happiness of a single word in education. And take positions that challenge a day of national opinion.

I have my personal opinion and I'm not afraid to say what I think about current issues, whether they like it or not. I do not want any with my detractors. Quite to the contrary. They made me become a man and now I know what I want and where I go. Yes. My grandfather was right. It is necessary to live and learn while protecting that we have of more beautiful: nature. Join with me in developing the party identity and culture of our nations traditions. I will not change and I do not disturb my views, whether political or economic, as they are in any essential way.

I test the duty of me to hold some has these doctrines which for a long time reject the forms of many convictions and which push me the every day to beat me for my origins and to defend the only right which exists here in this part this nation of the tribes Vikings. The fact that my own doubts were the result of my compassion for those who do not respect my blood made me develop a hatred that I should say pleasant because it plays to their ridicule. The faith of my followers scolded by a thousand times again and again and continue. It was these writings and this book so that I can improve the education of a great nation. The same one in which humans live for her and us for their own selfish inculcated by the industrial revolution which Chaplin mocked on virtually wholes films including Modern Times.

I have no opponent and I cannot have shame because I am the Viking symbol of fertility. I confess and I profess with the people and in the world of today that my justification will be increasingly large and the terms will be selected to save our empire of the world-wide crisis. I do not want us to be instruments of political crises as well through raged experienced as demonstrations without violence, not in any way represent a threat to the established order of a few ministers snug in their dens : as they are miserable !...

I am a chef and I'll never be a politician. My soul is too pure to be sullied by their wonders too sweet for me. They do not interest me. I will not sacrifice for you, gentlemen, my belief and my intrusive insolence for your blatant lies.

We need to position ourselves in a heroic debate and keep our honesty to fight in parliament to advance the order and not the first fruits of all petty bourgeois engulfed in the shadow of liberal capitalism gone well for so long that only European policies have still not understood.

I do not want any with my detractors. Quite to the contrary. They made me become a man and now I know what I want and where I go.

Yes. My grandfather was right. It is necessary to live and learn while protecting that we have of more beautiful: nature. The politician fighting for his mandate because he has his family not to feed but stuff like a goose for his own good. You represent, my friends, a vague recollection of a campaign where they still wash their hands of you have touched.

I want to be for our people so that public agitator that was Danton and led the people in power. It is enough technocrats. As they sang : «ah ça ira ça ira les énarques à la lanterne ah ça ira ça ira Les énarques on les pendra...»

Ah ! Ça ira, ça ira, ça ira,
Le peuple en ce jour sans cesse répète,
Ah ! Ça ira, ça ira, ça ira,
Malgré les mutins tout réussira.
Nos ennemis confus en restent là
Et nous allons chanter « Alléluia ! »
Ah ! Ça ira, ça ira, ça ira,
Quand Boileau jadis du clergé parla
Comme un prophète il a prédit cela.
En chantant ma chansonnette
Avec plaisir on dira :
Ah ! Ça ira, ça ira, ça ira !
Suivant les maximes de l'évangile
Du législateur tout s'accomplira.
Celui qui s'élève, on l'abaissera
Celui qui s'abaisse, on l'élèvera.
Le vrai catéchisme nous instruira
Et l'affreux fanatisme s'éteindra.
Pour être à la loi docile

Tout Français s'exercera.

Ah ! Ça ira, ça ira, ça ira !
Pierrette et Margot chantent la guinguette
Réjouissons-nous, le bon temps viendra !
Le peuple français jadis à quia,
L'aristocrate dit : « Mea culpa ! »
Le clergé regrette le bien qu'il a,
Par justice, la nation l'aura.
Par le prudent Lafayette,
Tout le monde s'apaisera.
Ah ! ça ira, ça ira, ça ira,
Par les flambeaux de l'auguste assemblée,

Ah ! Ça ira, ça ira, ça ira,
Le peuple armé toujours se gardera.
Le vrai d'avec le faux l'on connaîtra,
Le citoyen pour le bien soutiendra.
Ah ! Ça ira, ça ira, ça ira,
Quand l'énarque protestera,
Le bon citoyen au nez lui rira,
Sans avoir l'âme troublée,
Toujours le plus fort sera.
Petits comme grands sont soldats dans l'âme,
Pendant la guerre aucun ne trahira.
Avec cœur tout bon Français combattra,
S'il voit du louche, hardiment parlera.
Lafayette dit : « Vienne qui voudra ! »
Sans craindre ni feu, ni flamme,
Le Français toujours vaincra !

Ah ! Ça ira, ça ira, ça ira !
Les énarques à la lanterne,
Ah ! Ça ira, ça ira, ça ira !
Les énarques on les pendra !

Ah ! Ça ira, ça ira, ça ira !
Les énarques à la lanterne.
Ah ! ça ira, ça ira, ça ira !
Les énarques on les pendra.
Si on n' les pend pas
On les rompra
Si on n' les rompt pas
On les brûlera.
Ah ! Ça ira, ça ira, ça ira,

Ah ! Ça ira, ça ira, ça ira,
Nous n'avions plus ni nobles, ni prêtres,
Ah ! Ça ira, ça ira, ça ira,
L'égalité partout régnera.
L'esclave autrichien le suivra,
Ah ! Ça ira, ça ira, ça ira,
Et leur infernale clique
Au diable s'envolera.

Ah ! Ça ira, ça ira, ça ira,
Les énarques à la lanterne ;
Ah ! Ça ira, ça ira, ça ira,
Les énarques on les pendra ;
Et quand on les aura tous pendus,
On leur fichera la paille au c...,
Imbibée de pétrole, vive le son, vive le son,

59

Imbibée de pétrole, vive le son du canon

English Version:

Ah! It will, it will, it will,
The people say in this day ever again,
Ah! It will, it will, it will,
Despite all the rebels succeed.
Our enemies are confused here
And we sing "Alleluia!"
Ah! It will, it will, it will,
When Boileau once spoke of the clergy
As a prophet he predicted it.
Singing my song
With pleasure we say:
Ah! It will, it will, it will!
According to the maxims of the Gospel
Legislative everything is accomplished.
Whoever rises, it will lower
He who humbles himself, we rise.
Teach us the true catechism
And frightful bigotry turns off.
To be obedient to the law
All French will be exercised.

Ah! It will, it will, it will!
Pierrette and Margot sing tavern
Let us rejoice in the good time will come!
The French people at once quia,
The Aristocrat says: "Mea culpa!"
The clergy regrets that he has

By justice, the nation will.
By careful Lafayette,
Everyone will subside.
Ah! it will, it will, it will,
By the torches of the august assembly

Ah! It will, it will, it will,
The armed people always keep.
The true from the false we know,
Citizens for good support.
Ah! It will, it will, it will,
When énarque protest,
The good citizen nose laugh him
Without the troubled soul,
Always the strongest will.
Young and old alike are soldiers at heart,
During the war none betray.
Heart with all good French fight,
If he sees the ladle, boldly speak.
Lafayette said, "Comes who wants!"
Without fear of fire or flame,
The French always victorious!

Ah! It will, it will, it will!
Énarques with the lantern,
Ah! It will, it will, it will!
The énarques will be hung!

Ah! It will, it will, it will!
Énarques with the lantern,
Ah! it will, it will, it will!

The énarques will be hung!
If n 'not hang
They will be broken
If n 'not break
They will be burned
Ah! It will, it will, it will,

Ah! It will, it will, it will,
We had neither noble or priests,
Ah! It will, it will, it will,
Equality will reign everywhere.
The Austrian slave will follow,
Ah! It will, it will, it will,
And their infernal clique
With the devil will fly away

Ah! It will, it will, it will,
Énarques with the lantern;
Ah! It will, it will, it will,
The énarques will be hung
And when all they will be hung,
They will be driven the straw to c...,
Soaked in oil, sharp sound, live sound,
Soaked in oil, sharp sound of the gun.

18

18 November 2012

The leader must suffer all the consequences of his actions and take to the people, who asked him to be transparent in its political, economic and social visions. It must be consistent with the exercise of subsequent public actions and never fall into the errors of the essential points of his own role. The leader must be cement the trust of his citizens and accept what is his duty: to bring the nation to the level it deserves. It is true that political scoundrels do not respect nothing and like a song from a French author, Outdoor, which boasts the charm of opportunistic to the point that his jacket cracks on all sides after returned incessantly. And here is the image of these swindlers who praise us their merits and who do not deserve any more to be elected.

I did not want to appear and I had wanted for years to be behind the screen: the famous backstage. Do not ask me why ...

I therefore opted to make concepts transforming my girl-friends (top models, actresses or stars) to see how far I could go in the social media and its derivatives. I learned that unfortunately, when you create from scratch people who have actually no talent, have no moral either and you crush the slightest moment of weakness. It took me being thrown into bird food to understand and I began to exhibit my ideas around me in the most horrible attic of American prisons. I realized that I needed to create a committee to gather such as the Committee of Public Hi St. Just. I was looking in the books the answers to my questions hoping to cultivate the empty space was filled states of being.

I met various nationalist political groups, monarchists and regionalist who were all marked by the casualness of the political and economic nonsense duties of a company constitutes a nation. I do not want any with my detractors. Quite to the contrary. They made me become a man and now I know what I want and where I go. Yes. My grandfather was right. It is necessary to live and learn while protecting that we have of more beautiful: nature.

Find this Empire, Europe meant that I had to insist that parliamentary chambers to convince people that only a federal Europe regions could work. Because in any case the nations of Europe, it even Jean Jaurès, could not succeed. This is the reason that remained unanswered because there had been no other concept than to a single currency. In fact, policies we had taken on a journey of no return and no process because none had expected the plan. Yes! The Americans had primarily created a Marshall Plan.

But the European policies and technocrats preferred to make a currency without economic concept to plunge in the abyss because are they knew what they did by bringing us at the edge of the chasm and in this case they wanted the fall of Europe. Either they did not know what they did and in this case they should be prevented from continuing has to direct our administrations and that as fast as possible.

The existing of our nation depends on the decentralization of our institutions and the administration of our regions, in times past, were baronies, counties, duchies and principalities. Can in no way back on the past and that these gains were contrary to decide by any sense of the post World War II forces to promote the political power of some unelected who become because you trusted these lies in writing in books by the same people.

We go to a violent struggle of parties and unions who seek solutions in any case but excuses to divide even more Viking as if we were foolish enough to believe the lies after its parallel economies nations

What I want to say is that I believe in local politics and I remember the priest of Ascain, Basque country, who I admired and who organized around economic policy, artistic and traditional such diplomat and received from all its inhabitants a true recognition.

19

22 November 2012

The heart and the memory are my weapons which enabled me to dethrone the old world and to project me within the space of the rebirth. That even which came out within the menhirs of the era Viking and whose druids knew to project the odyssey until preachers write it.

It should be understood that for us Vikings, our interest lives in motherland represented by Freya which came directly from Asgaard to give to the man the direction of the life.

This native land which is expensive to us was the heart of all covetousness's at the point to want to test our passage over ground after the Second World War by inventing a past which is not true. Because only in the lie the diasporas could take pleasure in their ashes.

Attention I do not say that the history did not exist. But that it evolved. I will quote you for example Henri Guillemain who, wanting to give again with the history his noble letters, called truth, saw himself passing from large historian with rot, thus considered by his pars forgetting their own truth.

Since the 11th century, the Viking Empire had wanted to give his economic values the free exchange by giving free rein to trade in its first form of swaps. We had for centuries hand Preventable companies were manufacturing and trade between the expertise of these Gothic Celtic cultures and even if already the Empire of the Rising Sun we copied after the passage of Marco Polo, even when we were inventors and creative talents. Soap, for example, which was created based fat pig and embers of

traffic lights where you cook the pig. Ah yes. I must say that we love the pork and we get all pig except the teeth.

Domestic and foreign businesses were managed by a noble called Council House and we were discussing the price of wheat, the policy in terms of attack and judgment thieves. There was in a real serenity was moving the new order. It is true that we have never seen such artists as bright as our families. Bourbons and the Habsburgs were never able to match our workshops and artists. I should say today or for 3 republics was only passed from the hands of seedy and waste the executive, judicial and artistic. We see for example a 75 year old should not be allowed to work for more than 10 years as three institutions of French law. So what does power make? Well, they all suck, until you can no longer stand it and you return to the street as you have always done and they'll promise wonders. But this time, as some have heard, it is well and truly over.

Yes, because I'll be there with you in the streets to demand that before I even fair, did we want the truth because we know it is terrible. The truth is that for over 50 years, politics is sugar on the backs of workers and enterprises and that there is nothing more to take today. We live in the threat and injustice. We live in a Europe without creating, without service, with just one thing: the non-responsibility for its actions. When I stop at a traffic light that is not because the red light means annoy me! No, this is to let the waiting. It's called common sense, civic code or respect for oneself. Freedom ends where someone else's begins.

Politics is like art. It takes the best and not the opportunists who do not even know how to manage personal wealth. Mayors, deputies do not even know what it is that debt. And when asked to explain they are incapable; Sometimes they are outputs of style: "If I am to the direction of any town, I have specialists in each area. Ah yes! These same people who promoted French banks and live your money.

Do you know that in the U.S. today, when you have a minimum of 500 euros on your account, no account will the fees and bank charges? I'm not saying that America is better than us, but I say that people obey the law and if they do not they go to jail. Simple block or governor, everyone goes there.

20

23 November 2012

The centerpiece of the policy reinforces the tradition and elements of culture. This same identity attempt to save this great nation without flaws those above. These defects and let's talk! When the political world of the French right, for example, destroyed a power that does not exist ... Yes. How to give power to a person who is said to be neutral whereas if it was in the U.S., she would be in jail. Yes, sometimes I miss the American way and made me realize that we must judge our policies because they are thugs today. Why the U.S. would use to fill them to imprison political? Why do not we do it? Here's the answer: it is because we are not able to stand up to the forbidden while our Viking nation is always up against the enemies.

But what have we left to make our land that was given to us by the runes?

It is therefore necessary to centralize an organization as was the case for centuries as a form of decentralization of baronies also called regions or Länder, according to the language of our nation. But after all, this is the form that we expect to discover and define our vision of Europe.

Let's be clear and loud and wear our opinion is in high places and can no longer be overlooked or discarded in sandstone on their goodwill. I tell you, it's over. We will take up the reins of our nation and they can not play with our tribes for their own lust for power.

We need to create the nucleus of a Federal constitution of our nation to act on the domination of our Empire without having to justify to institutions that are supposedly there to ensure leniency policies that abuse the system. We must overcome these political habits as there is a climax: to be of the same party and have no difference apart lies and mediocrity. These people who think we are afraid to lead us. How can you trust a person who eats every night in 3 Stars far removed from the problems of the people?

I know what it is because I myself have made money and the scammers have made me believe that I existed. I began to live in palaces to not get out, only to first class, luxury cars and everything ... But I must say I'm happy because I'm not looking for money. I would even say that I do not want it. No, I'll live only for our nation and for her. This is the greatest gift that Odin has made me to be born in me the desire to fight me to the death to get our Empire in its entirety.

I'm with you, my brethren tribes to revive the greatness of our people that the numbers of people wanted gone forever. But we were there at the beginning of this world and we are here to close the lid of humanity. I will fight against this veil which means we have to and I wipe a sponge washing suddenly impurities from these rats.

Outside of our Empire they wanted to create in relation to ethnic nationalities trends to mimic our traditions of our clans. We do not want to mix us with these neighboring races, they are welcome on the Vikings land that has always been the land of exile and protected by Thor for the oppressed. But they never can get the blood flowing in our body and gives us the right to property and rights. I think of all tribes await the day when we have full power and dominate all of the new government.

We must recentralise the Odin guards to protect our territories and meet our leaders.

21

26 November 2012

The republic showed its true face with the death of the great figures who wanted, to come to power, to make use of the actions of the past. But seriously, I know that we must especially fight to fight the maintenance of the State. I will know, to take along my people has a centralization of the regions, to invest the codes in conditions of them that those are directed not responsible people who will not be able to grow rich with the risk to finish their life in prison in the same way that the United States holds their citizens. The fact that we have languages, which come from the norrois and of Latin, progressively created a so extraordinary and so rich culture that everyone is able to be understood, to sell qualities of the ones with the others. Our freedom comes from our principle of this difference which makes the jealousy of the world and of the races which have neither tradition, neither identity, nor culture. In any case, surely not like us.

We will unify within our nation all the tribes, with very strict laws which serve the people and not the worship of a person, as that was for longtime the principle. To stimulate the community for the gathering, to fight for the same principle and to put average the techniques to advance and live according to the flash of the red flag of the force. We need each one to set up the propaganda which you know so well because that starts as of the school where you are taught foreign rights which do not correspond with those of the requirements of the nation. Since tens of years the policy was in Europe overcome by services of propaganda which divided at the time of the cold war to let appear impostors. You understood you even. You felt that it occurred something and that there was a wolf in the sheep-fold. This wolf did not know, it is that behind the ewes the valorous shepherds hid who leave in the street because they lose their employment and that the state has no solution to cure it.

We need an absolute unity in the administration. I do not say "the administrations" but "the administration" because we must have an administration where the people who work there give has heart to find the ways to help the fellow-citizens and not to feel with the top as of laws. It will be necessary to re-examine as of now the operation of these principles of good citizenship.

I was always avid to know what had not been made and why. And to see there the mediocrity and the forfeiture of these dependent beings which have only one place: that which we will book to them. They were guilty by omission of the ruin of our great nation of our large Europe and we must judge them in front of courts of the people like in 1789. What will frighten them so much that they will flee with their economies hidden of Luxembourg in Switzerland. Money stolen to you, people of Vikings nations.

We are strong and durable. We are involved in all the quarrels and we are ready for an amazing way to support any drama without suffering severely for hope, inner fruit us since time immemorial rocks by messengers such as Merlin.

73

We can not accept mismanagement, maladministration and bad directions until all life has disappeared. Do not be dead on the low side, issued a 'trouble never satiated. Note us and become demonstrators as they known in 1968. Let us mobilize all the country and deprive of their rights. There is not other manner of proceeding only to drive out them. You see it in their ridiculous business of politicians who all condemns them without exceptions. We are an Empire made up of several people which was not maintained by the community of blood but by a handful of brigands ordered by foreign chiefs coming from secret cabins which live in the power of excess.

It is only by the common education of the centuries during, by common traditions, shared interests that this danger can be attenuated and that we will find the peace and the harmony of our Empire. Let us not forget the founding father of our ground. Let us not forget to turn us in nature and the organic one. Let us stop lying us to us same. We point out that we are the symbol of the traditions and the principles that the world envies us. If we cannot sell it then rent them, if they want the crumbs of them. Let us look at this torch floating on our suck and sing the anthem of the reconquest of our ground without fear and reproach.

22

2 December 2012

Neither the spirit nor the will be held on the mind, on the height of the successors and the tombs of our ancestors will be the emblems of the colors of our tribes.

A new era is born to revolutionize Europe and across the plains, the torches start to finish flare, torches of joy and victory.

Particularly for social causes and shoots by our ethnicities.

Revolutions have often been early struggle of races and not in the class struggle as they take to justify it. Because they have always had a single goal: personal power. The basis of the revolutionary uprising knows its origins in the sense of agitement people power that loses foot and suffers its agony in this lane masked with its ruins covered of its artificial crises led by the artifices of seasoned parliamentarians.

What did democracy mean? And more in this Western world where Orientalism became a requirement in the future of our society and its vestimentaux through a contrario of our provinces who do not understand and accept less.

A parliamentary representation requires order and the con-solidation of a common political language which must be called after the same brand of this symbolic system which is asserted in our occident.

Not to forget that the decline intervenes of the lack of order and thus of initiative of that which must carry out hands of Master our people and our nation. The reindeer's belong to that which convinced the chiefs of the tribes of Odin which assert according to them the diligence of only one and even undertaken, of an image which thorough Empire in a construction industry to be fought and advance even at the time of the difficulties. And to answer together in a direction even if it is false we will take this turn together and will circumvent the sour opposition to progress.

The instruction of a movement arrives by the sentence of a history which carried out these adventures and these details as if the blind men had been able to see the signs in the middle of their impossibility of a collective collapse. Proof of a will to destroy this nothing which burned the unpleasant one and which repents the hell indivisible vanity under beings.

I cannot lose myself because one would do of this book what I do not want and I want to go beyond what they can imagine box of the ruins to cause has our nations by treason of after war for the good of some vanities which continue and shock me more and more every day. I can react only in only one way in front of these beings which are not any more and resemble of it has basic animals court ...Although...

The federate states of the nations Vikings are for always the interest of the news of Europe and the only link between the past and the future to sit my political designs of the present.

What represents the Parliament today except for a bunch of people whose people do not even know its detractors and even less what they do there. Yes, it had well to be understood for the food. This place is indeed an appendix of the museum Grévin, museum of wax headstocks where one can see there characters which one does not even know the name besides. But here, it was that which the European policy which was there and to play a part so particular that it is necessary well to say. You understand there larger thing except for only everyone wanted to be a caliph has the place of the caliph.

23

5 December 2012

It is time that the first revolutionary indices leave the crypts and the tombs to flower again in all Europe, starting has to set ablaze the areas: from France to Hungary, until the fire took entire, pushed by the social classes which reject the political communities which lied and bathed in a bath of lust on the back of the blue-collar workers of unspecified condition

The European blue-collar worker cannot forget his origins completely and understand that it comes from the tribes which populated and made Europe this great nation which been jealous of so much so that everyone wants to plunder it to us, us to steal it to blow of swindles. The soldier who dozed of each one of us could not support any more to cook in this pot without the lid bursting, causing this revolutionary rising which had already washed our grounds of these parvenus who believed themselves once again on their premises.

I came to give again with this existence our faith and our honesty in our force and our courage. But also to delete forever these painful moments which drove out us of our houses at the point to pay even the price to die and to let itself catch in the chains of the malignant one.

The parliamentary representation does not exist any more. Its institution does not have more value than the door of my house and we must defy it as it defies us today by preaching the pessimism and *"I of foutism"* of these primates called appoint myself or other twaddle's which cannot even explain you what is the debt because they do not know anything of them even.

Tribes and clans how could you vote for impostors of which you do not know the names and who take wages, advantages and much more still on the back of your taxes and your labor?

Let us not expect the decline of our Empire whereas we are about to run. All these storms and these climate warming's are only the signs before runners of these monsters which threw our grounds grazes about it because they came like vampires to use all our heritage. Let us stop looking at the Indians of Amazonia as if the fate of our world depended on them whereas these same illiterate people are only the descendants of our slaves who are carried to the eyes of all in grazing ground to cause our unquestionable death.

It is out of the question for me to follow this disintegration and which I listen to the sentence history to shout with the miles adventures instead of destroying these unpleasant. I will enter gradually these courtrooms of keen politicians of their only desire for being elected officials of their famous gods whereas only the becoming good of the power of the Man and Highlander exists low here which takes the life to him to conquer its own research of eternity. I am counterirritated by these men who control us and who are only one band of cowards and cheap liars. I always understood at the point my dislike of the Parliaments and that their rubbish resemble cries and tears unchained on already lost causes. Yes, these men have only one fear: that to pass in front of the torturers as they do it today in front of you. It is necessary to cancel all the privileges of monarchy Bourbon and Habsbourg and to prevent whoever from going up on the right. It is necessary as of now canceling any compassion and sending to the dungeon the presidents and their ministers. Without rights and telephones, their life will not be any more that one hell as each fellow-citizen am live in the abysses of unavowed poverty.

I am for the freedom and the total abolition of the privileges. And if we made the revolution, it is not so that foreigners come to eat our bread and to drink our water.

The members of Parliament must give us an explanation because they are only our elected officials and do not have to gain more than all simple craftsman. They do not have to have unspecified privilege of mutual insurance company, at least not more than that of all the blue-collar workers. The equality of the policy must be a priesthood and not the requisition of the power like a room of the pars too often required by these same Sirs. A swarming mass people gesticulating, challenging one the other. Here what is the Parliament...A lamentable catch all swims about it, agitating its hammer violently, and making an effort sometimes by appeals for calm, sometimes by exhortations, to bring back in the tone a little parliamentary dignity.

I cannot prevent myself from laughing so much one would believe myself in the court of a re-creation of 5 year old children...

I believe in social democrat cohesion under the flag of plain Europe of the areas where each one would have a room which would give the good to be managed while collaborating in the effort of political good of federated Europe. The institution of the universal suffrage is made to recall these traitors whom we can ask a referendum, to stop the country of any movement such as May 68 and point by point to re-examine a constitution which is a vulgar joke written in the blood of a war which costed the life has million men, women and children.

There is no speech neither intellectual, neither economic, nor policy which comes us from the Parliaments. All the beautiful speeches are as many evidence as of their system which shows in the world a lamentable show and ridicules us all the more today.

Our grounds became swinging arms that nobody any more fears and of which nobody any more has interest because they sold the unsaleable one. What they did not belong it: our freedom!

24

8 December 2012

I studied, quiet, and yet bubbling of shame and hatred in front of this disastrous show of these lamentable elected officials whom you had chosen, more or less intelligent, me convincing of the tidal wave which it was necessary in this nation. Same which had pushed and supported Arab springs needed to be found in front of justice. Not that of the buddies! Not, that which will put them in ballot, in prison indeed out of on our premises.

A whole series of questions then arose my spirit.

I began to familiarize with the democratic principle of "decisions of the majority", bases of all the system, not without giving a serious attention to intellectual and moral value of the men, which the quality of elected officials of the nations forced a mandate to fill.

I thus learned to know at the same time the institution and those which composed it.

My consideration of the member of Parliament took shape in my spirit for finally seeing in him what was to be held about it in a state which should turn in the direction of a Swiss mechanism and not of an anarchy of the minis power which have the face of the decline of humanity. It is out of the question for me to mislay me and I want to constitute this capital of the nobility of duties which I must achieve for happiness to feel me again free.

Western Europe took the wrong way by seeing in the philosophical words a political concept good too often used by politicians in search of being able, too cowards to tell the truth, only their their truth. But what is there for example behind the democracy? The motdemoset the motcratoset absolutely not all that one told you during glosses by preaching you of the nonsense's the every day a little more grotesque. Not, the mot DEMOS means people and CRATOS means power. Thus power by the people or the power of the people or the power for the people. Finally thus as you see it, as many hooeys as one sold you during decades as besides the concepts which are attached to it such as freedom and the equalities which, as you see it, have nothing to do with the democracy but with the untrue plot orchestrated by the politico groups financial of the occident and the East in search of personal power.

This destiny which is mine vis-a-vis the policy was created by these groups which forced me to revolt me through these moments of hatred in which they plunged me to make me die. To make me disappear, because they were afraid of the word which I could evoke grace has this feeling to belong to the elected Viking tribes.

The error is to fall easily today into political parts in this Europe without conviction which is let exceed by its own navel-gazing ideologies and nothing has to sell except for stormy debates in front of the cameras in margin of their ground to make you believe has their reactivity.

I like the idea that the loads of the state are difficult to manage. But in this case, how to give them to people without formations and any knowledge of the letters and the ground? In both cases, there is a true disorder with the moral order politico which cannot apply so that Europe must and must be.

The Parliament takes as the bodies of the state of the decisions without knowledge of the problems considering which they received only from the parliamentary directives. But where is the problem on which I will return of course, it is how to make to apply all these laws without concrete means, without a police with a true power which answers has orders without a justice who answers the people of Europe and not with the politicians who direct us.

25

9 December 2012

A majority should not be made responsible because it does not have the idea of its responsibility vis-a-vis the nation; and it incurred direction of its determination to make responsible the acts for a government and of this chief which will have been selected.

The chief is the leader. He is that which carried out the group in a direction, but takes responsibilities for his errors, his failures and his victories. He is not afraid to officially say what its party thinks and what the people want their nations.

A chief it is leading which prepared a plan, a concept and which is held with this one. The statesman must convince by his smoothness of spirit and his oration by seizing the principles of hanging and of undertaking the decisions that it is necessary for to us at the moment when they are stated.

The chief cannot put the question to know today if it or not succeeds in determining the majority of an assembly to decide but to have this assembly to convince the members and federations of the party to help the chief in the direction to be only one and even voice because one cannot not be mistaken when the card of the opposition to progress is not played and that on the contrary one plays has to push the doors of the absolute truth.

Let us not leave the tumor engrain the body of the party nor more of the people as it is the case today and oblige to create a total medical action to remove this poison of cancer which causes to become gangrenous our people since too long.

We will have the clean hands and will release impossible dislike of this infamous being which then says the friend who is the enemy in all his power. I will take the poison of chemotherapy and would oblige our doctors to practice the intervention on each patient to leave there very partial of dead who could leave there.

I put a question to you: only once yes only once in your life did you understand an idea, a creation a concept before success is him even gained this one?

The action of genius must be an offensive taken only by that one even and taken again by this same mass which according to its guide and including whereas the only way for it to leave and follow it this genius which would fight until death for these people: such is the priesthood of their genius.

I refuse to go to flatter the policies which you know because I will be in this case the same one as these people of which I do not want to resemble as I do not want either to gain you by handshakes at the time of steps or other civilities which are not used for nothing and which are of nothing what we await from our people considering we want finally that the people of the nation Gothic Celtic Viking are only one and even voice in front of all the world administrations and dictate the laws which are ours and which dictate the world since the beginning of the existence of the man. Never we will fold in front of the foreigners such as Mittal. It is with them to put itself in front of us and to yield if not we will be obliged to direct us and to make them fold without any possible return.

Do not be stupid and stop waiting. We do not have anything to wait. Then let us take as we always made our courage and our honor. Let us block and come to power to change the face of our nation without listening to the conspirators. The guide must solve the conflicts with all the honesty which it owes. We must not forget that we have all of the duties towards the community and the obligations to preach the honor of our people.

Let us not be these politicians who are only cheap liars such of the robbers at the small week. Let us be worthy and take again the reverse of what the politicians want of us and what they want to make of us to use the weight of the responsibilities of them, carried by people bad not by themselves.

It is a man who builds and not a group. It is a man who leads and not a group. A chief, a guide is needed. That on which one can lean and acknowledge its weaknesses. A man who takes the solutions in the minute even where it touches the problem and not to pass by an administration of collective stopping's which see in work only zeal to obtain no-claims bonus at the end of the year.

It is extremely dangerous to see today that the members of Parliament try to draw the cover to create an authority which replaces the chief or obliges it to yield with this same authority on the right that it represents. This same mass that it disparages the every day with its superior airs. And I wait the day when I will see them as in the United States, model for all these conspirators selling off a sign "I am a politician, I am an impostor. I have stolen you, with you and my fellow-citizens". This day there, we will have finally gained oneself telling them democracy. But for the moment, it is out of the question which we recognize or respect the constitution as long as those which vote it preach in Napoleonean or bourbonesques privileges.

26

13 December 2012

I think that one needs a modern institution to reform a parliamentary sovereignty. It is what the press can fear because she makes fun of this assembly as long as this one is not ready to reflect and judge this independence which is due for him. One does not need only these monuments which represent the values of the French revolution and this cast and versed blood, pushed by Robespierre and Danton, fall into the meanness from these people who want to divert the direction even this symbol which should fight against the injustices and reveal a patriotic face and not of small encrusted middle-class men.

Europe is filled of a policy filled with cries and insults making it possible eels to slip and show pretty a peeling whereas they are there to only benefit from the end of a system in order to collect of them the parts damaged by the corrosion of the acids of the malignant one.

All want a place with the rows of untouchable which are those against which one cannot anything. Yes, I tell you. Louis XVI died and it is very well like that. There will be thus no row or of title to expect if you do not do all to gain them. It is necessary to destroy all the privileges of unspecified that it either has any price.

It is not because one puts a system places from there that one must keep it. If one lives through an economic system of insertion such as the RSA, in this case, the question is to do in exchange a work for the community and to become consequently irreplaceable.

There cannot any more be occupants of stations and stations to be convoyed in the state for the good this to hide with the sun. The consequences of these stations and people are always harmful and catastrophic. These manners at the Parliament are seriously dangerous and at the edge of the acceptable one, even of possibly correct.

The appointed chief will have finally to solve the problems and to position back an ocean without stopping with the care to return to the row its true value and not the perfidy of the combat of small chiefs seeking to still use the power to empty it its structures.

It is unthinkable to gain through bargaining. All that to have a temporal majority which cannot agree with the petty spirits and likely to create a political activity except standards.

How can one trust policies which resemble to merchants of mediocrities and whose public acts are non-existent and always return to the same sentence still and still? The famous one "I am not familiar with this case but it is clear that we should examine it in-depth". The files are not fishes and the elected officials are not soothsayers.

What is there at the assembly if not of the people who do not measure the responsibility for a life as a soldier in which you put in his hands your life to even defend this one? It is this feeling of confidence which carries high and strong the spirit gaining of joint work.

The fall as of these plotters is registered in the stars. While the druids envisage the bad paths to them, the Men as for them, will make by their weapons. The punishment to make pay the price of the shame which has emerges on these hearths in evil of consistency and libertarian spirit.

Cowardice. Here what characterizes the whole of our leaders.

That it then of all the attributes of the subordinates is who would have food for the nation and instead of that pervert in the scandal mongering of the kinds... Increasing is the intensity of the power and through the cries one will see a noble-hearted man approaching to make conceal the accomplices who wash themselves of any responsibility and who refuse the action of their acts. How a small hardly nimble professor can find himself to discuss with an avid entrepreneur under state and which does not understand.

27

15 December 2012

If it is imagined that the religious convictions are include with deep the human one, the political opinions are much stronger if they have a true meaning. They prepare the heart of the Man to his formation and his desire for belonging to a cultural propaganda to find in him the goal of the Graal: the cause.

The obstinate spirit of work on information can be taken in a manner of the simple communication or continues, to become about it the teaching and the model of the policy or the policies who manages and want in their hands this share of life and spirit. Attention not to fall to the hands from the harmful powers which glorify the malignant one by fear and shame of the total result of the world as a whole.

Is there a machine to educate the people which can determine with precision the most various aspirations of the sovereign state? Who controls the unverifiable one under a coat of betting and infamies, of which the persons in charge never are punished because protected from a layer of communities ready to justify the plots of the leading families which are foreigners and who try to melt themselves in the mass? They will be always discovered like these charlatans of Bonapartists and bourbonnais.

A press which continues to play the game of the state to get of a ridiculous detail a bargain of state. That it is a Twitter or a scoop of tax avoidance whereas one knows tens of years since what these collaborators of the power do who are ready to stripe very thought which could cause a problem of digestion to the bodies of the state.

Instead of leaving these names nothing to create a popularity to them that you, people bought without frowning, and who does not have a value the only word of its doors flags, opinions of the political leaders who decided to move on the right or on the left of the weak spirits. I cannot be associated with this bunch with lies and of calumnies which are poured by these powerful groups which believe being untouchable because they have relations and that they are led by bodyguard in the luxury car whereas they are only dangerous hooligans who will pay all their crimes like their conspiracies.

You do not serve as the newspapers to make there live your ideas of conspirators because one day or the other, these same press agencies will return you in the abyss of nothing which would be your only residence. These crooks feel invulnerable and on powerful loans with very to dislodge the least under the least part of Eur which would make them be to it supreme to deal a blow to all these victims than you are, for their only pleasure of destroying you without compassion, with laughter, howls of joy and pleasure as these enough stupid Romans of Néron to burn their city because only this show could be the symbol of the any human power on this ground and to exceed of them the gods, created by these same men.

If they do not find the way of closing your companies then they will go until denouncing them, to create of any part a plot with the disaster to liquidate. Yes, it is this setting with death which they like and not the production of which they do not have absolutely anything any more to draw because any from these billionaires earns more money on mines of conveniences and hydrocarbons that on pumps of blue-collar workers who are not used for nothing more than to carry out strikes. They find even a certain pleasure there of seeing the men bursting hunger in the street. If they deliver crescents, that surprisingly points out characters of Harlem who deliver the soup kitchens like famous Dutch.

Do not forget that they do not think as you and that their importance is not theirs quite to the contrary... Of course, most of the time don't you have anything considering coming and you will tell me which then are the alternatives? Is there at least? And well I will tell you yes. Indeed, today, everyone in France and Europe can keep its employment or to find one but one should not in this case vote for this policy of kinds which are not any competent. It is necessary to say not to any attacker whatever it is and to create a market economy and of protectionism in the strong and indivisible Eur with only one and even procedure to follow. But do you think seriously that these people that you have elected for more than 50 years are capable to direct though it either whereas they are not even able to direct a company or at least to understand operations of them?

28

15 December 2012

But after all, which became the public opinion?? Are there members of Parliament able to react, to engage, to fight and to have coherent speeches without needing to dig in sand to find non-drinking water and salted? One needs a leader who is exerted to make and to materialize the future of our nation because its only goal is the cause even of this ideology.

A library would not be enough to explain the details of convenient which is confined in the parliamentary assemblies and which re solder in the most extraordinary nothing where it will never be known if such or such appoints or senator actually were useful for though it is except for tapping under with the state and the privileges of the nation sometimes for him even... And sometimes in interests going even until protecting from the families known as of being able.

The policies tried to lie you by preaching values without rules such as the separate powers oneself saying and oneself saying impartial. For what that is used to as many elect people as one does not know who never do anything and who are unable to answer has some requests that it is? How you want that a deputy who never lived the idea of organization of a multinational or investment fund can take share has the defense of your interests considering which it the set of failures on which it was placed and that will not be able to understand is needed 3 has 4 blows to in advance be able to consider any opportunity. How these members of Parliament can decide and take directives without knowing the keys of them? It would be like giving a mathematical formula a 9 year old to child. Of course, the example is surprising and yet so much just! Finance is not invented and does not learn with the corner fire. We are not in detective series of 3rd zone where one knows already who killed which. We are in the establishment of the 21st century and we have in note European nation all that the world wishes and envies us. Then why aren't we able to answer the absolute truth?

Which is the reality of these various administrations which refer constantly to being validated by the members of Parliament who have the round back to confirm non-existent acts in the same decisions of the wills of the collective lie. These governments do not need more to ask though it is at the Parliaments and use of it the system only in the event of major force to sit their decisions. Thus I ask you where is the balance of power in these cases.

Do not mislead you there. The government is responsible for all but the members of Parliament also, because they should be put in public indicter's like made deputies such as Just Saint with the aggressiveness which it was necessary for this revolution to impose and take the initiative to cancel the privileges and to put in front of the people and the nation these oneself saying leader to answer of their life with their blood of the truth which it is to take of the political directives. This same revolution of which all today invite to remember whereas this one was done in a blood bath which did not stop any more in the name of the freedom and whose impostors claim themselves whereas they all would have been guillotined considering speed to finish of it Committee of the Public Hello directed under hand by Robespierre, extravagant and obstinate political character ignoring the good and having for conviction only the virtue this one even which given it in front of to the point calling some with the terror which feels in its words of an anthem reflecting the violence of a war carried out for the image of a man.

11th century with today, the Vikings knew to bring to their people of the traditions to give the fruit of it through their laws like wanted it William the Conqueror to embellish the life of its subjects and including the need to share in the unit the law, to respect it and enforce it at the cost of first of all judging those which must enforce it that they are politicians, civil servant or all authorities to make apply these principles of the directed authority.

But it is true that since the American revolution, the idea to have a representation of the hétéroclite government had strongly given to the people a healthier but unfortunately lamentable impression of perfidy which became more and more a concept of nonsense which wanted to make believe that an universal suffrage could be a decision of the people whereas that represented a hostility even stronger which points out the well-known expression to me "to move back for better jumping".

To solve problems, and in fact the problems of the people of Vikings nations, is not close to everyone. It is necessary to be plunged in the diversity of the problems to solve and select them in groups, to form concepts which will be able to answer the future visions of the whole of our desires. It is necessary to create a forum to collect the requests for each one and to analyze them to answer and give whole satisfaction it to our people of culture and identity.

29

20 December 2012

The future of a state, of a nation does not have anything part of poker. Even less than one game of caster which is played between aficionados in a casino. The nation is not sold with highest offerer because one cannot sell what is not with us. All these members of Parliament are the irresponsible ones who would have to pass before the Committee of the Public Hello of Just Saint to answer not of not to have made their crimes but anything. Because it is the problem there! In this large Europe, the policy does not do anything to derogate from the famous Napoleonean code with which one should make only one thing... But I am polished too much to say it. Most of the time the members of Parliament do not have knowledge. But they do not have either the intellectual possibilities to take directives on questions which escape to them completely and which leu pose problems of conscience considering that they do not know how to manage them. One needs an uprightness in the state, the nation, politics and economics of tomorrow. The people of Europe need the good citizenship and the respect of others while starting with their members of Parliament and their police who must be a front the people and the state. There is no more leader and I see it the every day with the way in which the people lead what is a real scandal and a shame for the collective conscience. The decision is deserved together if not it is necessary to go on a desert island. It is necessary to stop believing that a law can intervene on an immediate effect of the use of the economy of the policy when the civil servant do not make them respect because they do not have chiefs whom they can follow and of which they can be proud.

Let us not fall in the honesty which represents the silly thing and rather into the true image from oneself even through the values from the past for a future shining this very day. Let us not wait and make the decisions which change our world immediately. In less than 4 years I will raise our nation with the row of first and the whole world will turn to us because will be we the images that all we will copy by protesting our songs.

It is necessary that the members of Parliament are guided by a party which votes in a state of cause for purpose to release to the maximum the truths which are subjected to him at the time as of votes. The committees must be there to answer and train these members of Parliament and to give them an experiment to promote within the ground a concept which will be the same one from the top of the machine with the bottom of this one if there are a top and a bottom however, in a certain way of imagining an image of a traditional party. One cannot let any more answer the executives of the policy which are believed untouchable because they were it until our days. Today, it is the blow of brush expected by all the social classes and policies.

Let us be honest and look opposite this majority elected people being caught for the notable ones with their small desks of zero which they are indeed. And I will not be afraid to tell them that they must now leave and not to return more. These people make you believe since too long that if they left it would be the rout, chaos. But which is it now? Isn't this chaos, the impossible *raison d'être* and the total destruction of construction? Yes these zeros are moreover limited to believe than they are essential to our life. Nobody is essential; it is necessary to go essential to be it and I cannot say that the policy of these 65 last years were marked by the fact of being essential, but by that to be a miserly nullity of compliments, egoist wanting to have the world with its feet the such dictators whom they attended and became even friendly about it so much it is good this power to make and demolish.

You know well that all the decisions which were made and of course the bad ones for a country are not the responsibility for anybody. And well I want to be responsible for all that I will engage for our nation and I will make as of the first times acts which will make our largest nation of the world because we are only and single. And for this reason all want to come on our premises when they are rich of course.

30

21 December 2012

The political world preaches the democracy. But which is it today if it is not a word used too easily by the dark or poor spirits? I cannot any more accept the members of Parliament of today who come from abroad to teach me lessons and learn what the French revolution represents. It is by fear that we will be able to oust the weak ones and to uncover the cowards, because only could remain the defenders of the rights of our nations Vikings, Celtic and Gothic and not be weakened by European antagonisms more.

The Parliaments live and vote to the detriment of the people of Europe and still do not understand the regionalistic quality of the separations for a great empire... For the Empire.

That it is Normandy, Transylvania, Catalonia, Basque Country, Brittany, Sicily... All have the right and the duty to organize regional committees making it possible to make decisions faster as well economic as political and of course military, especially when islands are threatened by an excess of immigrant coming from one oneself saying new democracy as one wants to make us hear it. I do not want to be any more ashamed of what I am and I will not be weak in front of members of Parliament who reduce our people in slavery since too long. It is time for us to begin again what is with us and not to ask whether they are of agreement or not. But by the ballot boxes to recover in our campaigns. We should not any more pay the expenses and organize only one and even Europe which lives only through our traditions. It is this identity which carried out the people to revolt and take up arms to live in the growth of a patriotic liberalism often badly understood where some can find there aspirations erroneous.

We are not old Europe but a nation in charge of History lends to reconquer the world and which at all does not need the others but which carries out the world. This ground turns thanks to us. We are the creativity, the spirit, the vision and the bursting of an image constantly in search of a knowledge to make which characterizes us. Today what can it arrive to us of worse when one sees tearing of each one and the mediocrity of those which control us at the point to be made write their text so much they did not take in question the concept which should animate them and are only puppets with the service of groups which in fact directed and are spirit to be made eat by others which want a share of this appetizing cake.

The intoxication of a one day victory cannot be the apotheosis of a nation but the enthusiastic clamors of the people show at which point the ideology and the practice of a leader can be the way which leads to the resurrection of the policy and the action of this one on its own economy as long as on its vision of foreign growth.

What is it spirit to occur? Well... All these governments which follow one another lead us to the ruin. And the worst, by all the ways which they can find. Then you will tell me but which their interests well the groups which are behind their make believe has important rooms in the future state of a new world order which would be directs by companies not secret but elitist or to return it is necessary to have certain assets in the hands.

The members of Parliament are the culprits whom you seek because they glorified governments which had only one idea at the head: that to be maintained with the power to control a pseudonym authority however betrayed thousand times and using all the facets which could all the more lead them to control these poor spirits.

In fact, I will make you a comparison with the media. A few years ago, a number of poor consequent returned in the media and the leaders liked them because they were quite simply leather rounds. The problem it is that since this moment, there is neither creation, nor innovation and we bathed in the reconditioning of products already given loans with employment. I will not quote the person who will recognize herself and who told me that one day, in its recording company, it had made listen to a music on which a poor art director had told him that it should take again "some notes here and there".

And of course, this person was going to be carried out when she preferred to go to live her weekend end on her side, returning to the label Monday and making play back the same song. Without nobody touching there, the art director gratified himself of this new version which he thought of being a tube. Here exactly, with the image of the economy, which is the policy.

31

24 December 2012

The independence and the freedom of the power of the members of Parliament are often threatened these groups ready to use illegal means like true oppressors. In fact, I am not there to preach for a state but for the defense of the traditions of the races Vikings, Celtic, Gothics which made Europe this great nation. I came to recall it high and strong without complex none. The equality is not in the middle of the debates considering which it was never respected in some manners that it is by which conch of these groups which, feeling lower, preferred to bring back it besides to a state of exile in ways often quite cumbersome.

Slavery does not exist on our premises and never existed in the sense that certain tribes or certain people of other continents want to use it well still today. The right of the Vikings takes precedence over the right of the policies and of the members of Parliament whom we have and we must recall them in a strong manner to remove us forever from these leaders of imposture's and galures.

Our fight with happiness was generated by our cultural identities and our rights to live in a perfect equality between men and women and without artifice in unspecified manner that it is.

I am ready to fight for my existence and ready with any sacrifice for this freedom preached on several occasions by our tribes of the crusades with the fratricidal wars. I ask you to rectify your heads and to put to you in conflict towards the people who deserve the judgment of our fathers. I do not want any to intend to speak about change but quite simply because of finding in my roots my ground which respects the values of my grandfathers. I say it: that any person who is not in agreement with our tribes has the choice to start from on our premises. I say well "on our premises" because it never was differently. The tribes gather under the standard of the runes to be only one and even armed opposite chaos and I will be there to hold up this standard to the last breath of life which would not know that you believe. Because my death was already pronounced and I am there to achieve the way of the man who I am by the will of the free men and proud who we are. Tribes! We join together around only and even idea and beat us against imposture

The laws of the theorists only exist to destroy you and make you lose conscience. Look at what you became: lambs at the point to authorize to pay taxes for a house, a family heritage that your large parents already paid. Isn't this the means there of stealing you and of preventing you being owner and from disuniting your goods between brothers and sisters?

Our dynasty Na not need to reappear because it is there and well there. It was certainly sullied by policies who preferred to grow rich rather than living on their true commitment but the past is the past and we do not need to still remake still and the same errors. It is necessary for us now to raise the head and to fight in the same direction for a policy for an economy and a finance: ours.

It is necessary that in full Parliament one intends the voices to rise and to acclaim the true vision of the world renewed and who believe in only one and even doctrines to be able to live in this harmony of joy which will fight side of large Europe. That where all proud because will be finally gathered to us around our myths. Proud to look with far these people without cultures, identity and any tradition.

Does one need a war to find us? Is it necessary to let make the industry groups which expect only the wars and the economic crises to gather us? We gather and beat us today to make our great nation this large Europe, this dynasty centers world.

32

24 December 2012

Idiocy my friends of these policies who live in abundance and allow themselves to exploit the classes middle-class and working are completely postponed and indeed finished. They do not have any interest in any case... All these impostors are only one afraid: it is fear to lose their assets. They give each other a right of reserve which enables them to rebound constantly to allow itself to be Masters about it. Let us be honest. You absolutely did not understand what occurred during the change of the purses of the year 2000 and how the markets of Europe were made destroy by the NYSE and the purses of Hong Kong and India. Even less on this Eur which was seen being born without constitution and model, instead of repairing true indices of economies such as for example the barrel of oil in Eur and not dollar then in Eur what calls upon an enormous money dead loss. Then you will tell me. What did they thus make these members of Parliament during this time when were to fight to protect the Eur, the stock market, the collateral exchanges? And well nothing! Because how can a person who does not have the knowledge of this work start to imagine a strategy? For example, imagine a plumber and ask him to repair an engine of harmony. And well it is a little the same thing.

It is necessary that the mass wants to move in the same direction to triumph and engage the fight necessary to block and release for the good of the nation. The problem today of the people, it is the comprehension which the social one can be set up only if the finance strategy and economic is directed by a policy itself carried out of face by only one party and only one leader. One cannot go in three different ways to arrive at the top of the mountain when it is known that one goes until in top and bottom and circumvents it.

The middle-class classes always fought on the back of the blue-collar workers and of the small employers to give him any value, even if this one knew well that there was no exit except for that of the elections can be.

It is necessary to sit a troop of partisans to gain not by step the voices of the voters and to create through this sway in the crowd a true organization which compromises all the strategies which had been carried out against our people.

The character of these personalities was of course carried out with a serious injustice. But let us not be we there any more and it is necessary that we can act as a tactician.

To conquer is of course in the blood of my entrails and I have same blood of course. But I cannot invite to conquer the fact of wanting to find its grounds and to find in his center one and only even tradition as a mother in whom one lives!

I cannot look at my ground becoming arid and seeing it trampled by non-believers, carrying me in a violence without a future where I will on the ground throw the armed wing of my brothers Vikings, Celtic, Gothic until Freya takes to me in its arms until I find the direction of nature. That of Asgaard.

My political consideration is made of my desires for living and for arriving at the more high summit of my heart to feel me filled in ego that the ground waits of my vision to be: a man respecting the values of human whose blood runs in me and the tears which run my eyes see only the beauty of a satisfied world makes truth and of transparency.

Raise and have the faith as I have it in you to do of this world that which you want, where the assistance and the division are the spirit of our body and that we trusted only one front the eternal fir tree. This sap and this blood interfered forever for the beauty this single ground which saw the world being born and growing. The will of the combat of the people Viking is concentrated by the attraction of a movement to make disappear its adversary which was declared as tel. Never a Celt will not preach the battle but never it will not stop as much as one of both will not have left the territory. Because we were born under the animal sign and our behavior is that. The massive power of the shock is quite real today. It is the moment to elect our chief to fight and live the conviction that our enemies multiple and are varied but that they will not be able to sit down and make disappear our cause.

The movement paganism is a manner of having continued the symbol of our fathers through traditions which they believed to be lost but that we kept at the bottom of our hearts.

IV

Europe

33

30 December 2012

Old Europe and young Europe...

I returned on December 24th, 2009 to Europe. I was filled with wonder to see this so strong and large continent, so incredibly eager to keep and preserve its artistic and artisanal wealths, but I was afraid. Who were all these people eager to destroy this continent and why? I felt like one prewar time with ridiculous wages. I wanted to ratify all the towns of Europe the ones with the others to create this assembles areas which would make it possible to make fold all the leaders of the current policies which had ruined our continent in all full knowledge of the facts, with an only aim of piling up the results of benefit on their reciprocal in tax havens out of Europe, of course.

I saw the ruin in all the directions of the term threatening this empire which still resounded in my head like the cradle of humanity. I walked, blind man to find in this public opinion the necessary support with the radical change which was to give only one and even direction and a leader to preach the ideas which, being based on the past, would become the success of our existence of the present and this near future.

I saw how to raise our continent in 4 years and how to make the first world power of it. Because in fact, we had very to be it.

All my life, I traveled around the sphere and created a marketing in each place in which I passed, so much so that the groups were enough animals to follow me and to invest money, even over very short periods of annual profitability, it has to say not more than one month.

The feelings of the people were lost in the silly thing of the journalists, the policies and the surveys carried out by Mafias. Yes, I call them Mafias even if officially they are called the groups of investments or the national multi. It is necessary to break and answer in a firm way.

I saw that unfortunately the trade unions had them same changed good and opened out in the lie of liberal capitalism while making accept their members whom they were going to fight. I do not need to sit me with a table with policies to dictate only one manner to them of making turn the companies. And I will prove to you throughout this political book that the European companies and Frenchwomen do not manufacture here any more for a moment already and dare to grant the "Made In France" whereas it of it is nothing. It is necessary that the working world and employee understand that the only means for Europe of being is to break these racketeers who have of cease only to garner billion for their own person and whom they make absolutely nothing for the Vikings people, Celtic Gothic and that they hate the traditions of which they do not make by part. I want to see proud owners to be beside the power to decide and garner dreamed of Europe free and quite bearing, leader of the worldwide market and trainer of the ideas and concepts for a sure value and pure.

These big bosses are bet them company and must be treated as it should be: like traitors with their country, their continent. Because the greatest infringement of the law and indeed the tax avoidance reprimanded in certain countries like the USA for a minimum of 20 years from firm reclusion without grace and restitution of days in less than sentence. Tax avoidance shows that this person wanted to fly since the beginning and that this loss of money in the economy of the nation is the ruin of our company. As besides the foreigners who come and to assert a right of allowance for, themselves, to create an escape from money which plunges our continent in problems regulated for a long time by the first world power. Then what! It would be necessary that are the best only others. We are not imbeciles who believe in the worship of golden calf and we must drive out all these poor who are only to weaken large Europe.

34

1 January 2013

The hour came from alliances between all the European areas to find this large Europe and to build the 21st century, us who sums in year 10195. Spiritual century or century you will not be... All the regions must be subjected to doctrines which are shared already around an only political party which must establish an economic and material guard to fight in the ideas of a great nation higher than any other continent.

The continent of Europe was to establish a common policy and to continue until the end to sit an economy based on acts and not on laws controlled by poor members of Parliament in the pay of groups which assert the end of Europe by calling it "old woman Europe". Whereas is what that wants to say when, in front of me, I see only countries without culture, languages or vision?

The lack of diplomacy was suggested by policies which resemble more to racketeers than with men of conscience ready with very to build and live with the likings of a freedom acquired after being itself beaten for these grounds.

Width of our people warlike, which was keep silent under the influence of these traitors who had sold what cannot be sold, in fact our grounds because they belong to our traditions. We cannot sell what is and will be always the law of blood.

Europe has a goal: that to give to our nation, its tribes, a life which they can hope for. It must live because it is the cradle of humanity. I card-index myself of what one tells me. They are ashamed lies to make our Europe a ground either scorned, or declining. it is enough Sirs. I ask you as of now answering in front of courts drawn up by the people – by these clans – which will come to ask you for accounts and whose sentences would be much harder than you imagine.

Imagine how it is now almost impossible to nourish a European army! Then one tells you by beautiful sentences that one in does not require, that it is not the important one. But what is important then? I ask it to you. Do the people have to pay for the gifts and this life offered to the members of Parliament: between official cars, apartments of function and dinners to the expenses of the princess who is only your sweat?

We must reproduce between us and agree on a settlement. We should not any more accept on our territories that tenants and give restrictions as they do it on all the continents. The diagram must be simple and we must regulate our laws on the laws of the others.

Thus if it is difficult, even impossible to assemble a company and that there exists an imperialism, we must make the same things without pity nor compassion none to save our richest and powerful continent of the world.

The time of the constraint is finished and the Marshall plan buried, like the treaty of Versailles. The more no foreigner will control us and the more no system will be able to dictate our will to us. We vote for Europe free and full with life until the end of our destiny.

The value of the individual for us people Viking, Celtic, Gothic represents the eternal wisdom which makes us these men painted of blue and ready to fight with sword and launches. Our race is largest and I am happy to carry it high and strong. I do not have any gene of what I am and to preach, through my image, the every day, my ideology.

With the turning of the way, I see only nations which were high in the total obscurantism, at the point not to know their clean traditions more, to know even more of which tribe or which clan they comes. It is necessary Re-to cultivate the European people and to show them that our traditions are jealous of so much so that they ordered, after the second world war, to make them prohibit by our leaders of then who were not that sold in the pay of is saying allied. Those even which were cynical non-believers.

The history of Europe was rewritten so that you do not know anything so much so that Stalin had become the small father of the people about it. He which, with its political office, invented the concentration camps. Let us be realistic. These books of history of the schools and colleges made it possible to use and promotionner against truths, and even of the lies to indoctrinate the world with the constraint of golden calf, of the money of the dollar of the foreign financial markets.

35

9 January 2013

One day I will see proud Europe of its people and existence. I say it today to you. If they want the destruction of our tribes, it is that they know that we are strong people. We are this race which made Europe an indestructible power. These people which today revolt and take the weight of the life to fight and make float this flag of the tree of life.

Where is one the limit when speaks about the ground of my ancestors? The people of our nations before are very dedicated today to their destiny and must find their cause and their goal to live for this same way. That there even which makes them it utility to live and not the symbol of a company without roots which plays in between supermarkets and motorways has an encumbered air of a sour nullity which clinks between two mountains until "the sky us falls on the head" as said our ancestors.

We arrived at the ultimatum disparaged for a long time by large scientists who preached already the fact that the world could not be left there and that one did not control humanity. But especially that which is not used for nothing, that you can see to come to beg all the day, fruit of a Mafia foreign of these people who understood that we had, in Europe, the donation to accommodate the oppressed people. Those there even which make use of our manners to destroy us. But here. They do not know the teaching nietzschéen which preaches the values and our present, through three examples, how we must react; By quoting the two first which are against the pride even of poverty human due to the tender of the religions that we let us loathe more than all considering their indigence to make reign the order and the truth.

Example:

A beggar is in a front of a church.
- First option: you want to take the blame off you then give him three pennies.
- Second option: you make pretence that there does not exist to exonerate your compassion which is however quite present;
- Third option (the good one): you flank a thrashing to him and return it at his place to blow of pumps in the mouth.

Once again, Friedrich Wilhelm Nietzsche shows us how it is hard, after an education made of under heard, to answer the pure and absolute truth. To protect its territory against this beggar who is actually a swindler, a robber, who came to mow you to treat you of impostor and robber in its turn. I remember, a few years ago, to have met simple people whom I had met randomly and whom I had had desire for helping to avenge me for others making the same trade of promoter in the New Yorkean night. The latter, at the end of the accounts, stole me and then treated me of robber I wondered what I was to do. Was I to lead these men to the guillotine as would have said Robespierre? Well surely! In any case, it is obvious that they were not American. They had come without paying, which I did not know before because I did not even have idea that one can return on a territory without paper (or with false paper) for the simple reason that I would never have done it me even.

I will tell you with the wire of these pages "why" of my battle to save Europe and with the fact that all the people who say that our countries of Europe are condemned are them even paid by groups which want to make us disappear. Because we are the only rampart with this humanity and will destroy we them because we will save water and tornadoes our nations which answer only one idea. That which Odin is stronger than all and than we are the men of the forest.

The races Vikings, Celtic, Gothic must remain, live and generate the revival of our Europe. Let us let the other people without cultures to kill each other. We want neither to return in conflict nor to take sides with them because they are not our tribes of Europe and do not correspond to the commitment of our true solution of the world.

36

10 January 2013

Nature decided and announced its choice.

It turned to us on several occasions. How, people without cultures, you can follow our slaves and go until the end of the world with them without any knowledge, without any culture and knowing or at least knowledge?

Balance will be done by average much the largest than you cannot imagine it. And Marline laughs at you today, because whoever does not know the Excalibur sword cannot understand the faith in the power of the dragon and its force forever. The races of our nations will make very to sit and ensure the ground of our forefathers.

Nature does not know the political borders of these countries which are said civilized or give itself words of democrats. Not, she knows only the sap which runs in the blood of each Viking

The game of the forces turns around the sphere while we lose our true goals. We are not there to resign us to save our lives of a well of despair. I say it today to you. You have, people of the nation Viking, Celtic, Gothic, the noble task of living and making live our cause. Knowledge and to announce it.

Our territory must be protected. The gift of Asgaard to have offered this ground to us of which everyone envies us the beauty is the fruit of the life that the every day we can drink and crunch with full teeth. It is the fruit even of the will to share this paradise together living here.

That made too long that groups tried to establish ideas to destroy and make flee our people. These lies are only libelous remarks which have one face: that of imposture and the right to steal us fruit of our ancestors who fought to protect and save this ground which does not belong to us and which our Odin father gave us to preserve it and to give him all the support which nature can need.

It is absolutely necessary to save and help the every day this peasant class and to encourage it to develop this work which makes of our best products market and shows once more that Europe can live without the rest of the world. We do not need moreover these areas to which we brought more than the knowledge: the serenity of which they did not even know to appreciate the pips nor the means of us of thanking some.

Agriculture is the base even of Europe. When our food is seen, we do not want to resemble to these barbarians of the other continents which live between the products recreated by machines and hormones which one does not know the consequences yet.

But Europe, it is also to be to trust of its institutions. Which is they so not its armies, its Police and its Justice ?

It was necessary to center and bring a chief to lead this great nation and to rediscover our people odinists for the greatest pleasure of these institutions in evil of being because damaged by these poor and poor policies which made them leprous executive power and which can nothing any more make except for waiting and obeying the orders of impostors come to redouble their personified silly thing.

I want to recreate a constant force with laws and rules. We need the total order without any reflection of some kind that it is. It is necessary for us to put at the step these enemies of our people which think of playing the malignant one. But not with me. I will give them so much evil with being which they will start from them even by beseeching and imagining all the nights to see me to drive out in them this malignant of which I found the artful thrust. I will be the happiness incarnated for all Europe and the evil for all those which sullied my way.

I will support all the police authorities and I will give them the order to give again the human face of serenity. I want Europe where the flights do not exist and or one does not need to close the door of at home because one knows the punishment has those which would dare to pass in addition to the commitments that I will have made in front of the people of the nations of Europe.

37

17 January 2013

The future of our size is there, in front of us. In three months, I will rectify our country. In 6 months, it will have left the crisis. In two years, it will become most powerful of the world and will dictate in the world its requirements without listening to theirs.

One cannot escape our destiny. It is obvious that we seek to live in harmony for the happiness of our people and that we dream of world peace. But we must be a little realistic and look opposite the truth a quite complicated life for us, human, alive in a company weakened by the pseudonym media ready with very to make you believe that you are prisoners of religious stereotypes...

Certain groups spoke about Europe which would be propagated through the third way for the future of plain Europe. The west and the east were to gather conditions and concessions and what could be more normal than the spirit of a family which fought for the present of a tradition.

I will progressively reconsider the points which will make the unit of our people, referring to me to the history of this line which traced a continuous line since the 8th century with today... We must in addition find an industry and a world commerce because we are the center of all the world creativity.

We do not need the others. It is out of the question to sell off us and we must impose our style to them and to not to sell our knowledge them to make and in fact to rent to them.

This development of the business would not be easy nor rapid if we do not change the idea of new Europe. We must throw to the refuse a whole state of worn parts as we do it in our house and we must empty our wall cupboards.

Unlike an industrial rise, Europe must restructure itself to take again the advantage of these markets which were lost by the poor politicians. Those there even which ruined our Europe and continued to use the most turbid methods to draw from the profits on income taxes your and to help themselves in the cases of the countries in the process of development, under cover of companies screens in authorized tax havens as is represented by the Benelux countries which must end in a transparency that we will oblige with these countries which refuse the authority of our great nation.

I want to build with you a large fleet which will direct our people to be able to even fight against the lost fights created by people without any respect of them and ready to ravel itself with the least problem. When Europe can take the route of a strategic economy to control its to provide and financial reflection and to project its new generation in a world of order and culture where the assertion to be grace of the conquest was finally strewn with right and vision: nonutopian progression of a quite real world.

The various countries of Europe must give again in Europe this regional heritage which returns to us more extremely and more alive in a European territory where the single policy multiplies in various actions of this energy which is propagated only in our great covered nation of a Utopia where, only, we will reign without needing to repeat with our guests who they are only guests and who constantly a passport can be abolished in consequence of a bad conduct and lack of donation in our community and our large continent.

There will be no excuses and I will be obliged to recall to any person the codes if she does not behave with best self even in any object of legal and speculative conditioning. An economic and peaceful conquest can be non a complete direction of a world in perdition.

The doctrines and professorial of the history wasted the training of the men and our role is to redefine the limits of them to understand and evolve within strong Europe a such great nation that this one represents...

38

19 January 2013

If America, at least the United States of America are the model of the democracy, then we must imitate them on the various methods, that it is in justice or the economy, while following to the letter their manner of acting. In this case, nobody of the United Nations will be able to return on what we will do considering it will be in the worthy respect of the rights of Washington DC.

Then Europe will reappear of its ashes: no people better than the European tribes better nor more brutally prepared its economic conquests by the sword, and did not defend them more resolutely.

The policy is there to sit our economic conquests and to make use of any plot of land in our interest. Once again, the man does not live for him but for the nation. The idea of freedom was to use in the bad term and became it "to do what one wants". And well not! One does not do what one wants when one wants. If you want to live under this method then you go on a desert island and good wind! But today, *that is to known as you what I make for my people, my country, my ground?"* This life, this body does not belong to you and not been part of a whole and this one even which makes us different beings because our naps directed by our traditions. Recently, a person told me that he did not like that I use the word "race" to speak about Europe. And well, it is however what we are. And of impostors such as named, the members of Yalta – Churchill, Stalin, Roosevelt and the funkier de Gaulle – wanted to make you believe that you belonged to a worldwide economy called ultra liberal or communist globalization and that you must forget what you had learned and especially the word of the Aryan race... Yes Aryan. Whereas certain legends were propagated in the world, the symbol was to be confined by a war of which you had only the short ones and who were done to destroy our people. One day, at the time of one of my dinners I caused in a nice way an Indian friend so that she says has all those which were around the table which she was Aryan and proud to be whiter than the others. The white people of skin were confused and outraged of one let us blaspheme going against the principles inculcated of Aryan of the Second World War. Once again, you awake and recall you that one lied you. You confined yourselves in the lies of a society based on the swindle of a world where you agreed to be the slaves of men loose and stripped of any political envergeure.

Europe needs today an armament like army worthy of this name and to show that even to the sound of sword and to deepest of our freedom often interpreted by the kilt than I carry in tribute to thousands of soldiers who died for our justice. We will protect and we will fight for our values. We will once again kill the flame of the dragon come to play most extremely with us.

We are not mercenaries even if, for some, we resemble to barbarians with our dyed faces of blue to defy the enemy. But we will draw with deepest of our blood the sacrifice to give to our people the unquestionable victory. But this time, we will crush those which wanted to defy us, the such chartre Norman-Sicilian.

We are brutal, in the will of the combat. These groups forgot at which point. But they quickly will remember or their parents will tell them because we did not have to be awaken. I want to die for this ground which is Europe and from which I am happy to represent against the enemies of the large and very powerful state.

Any policy knows well by me seeing that I will not bend like the others in front of them and that I am able of very to save my people because only account for me large Europe. I was born to defend it. I am not afraid of the press or the satirical newspapers because if they see in me a man of convictions. Then it is that they will have understood that I need neither money, nor of being able. But I need to be able to look me in an ice and to tell me: "this ground was given to me by Odin and I am proud". I will fight for the honor of the Gothic people Celtic Vikings and I to look in the eyes whoever will want to cope me by expressing to him what this ground represents for me: freedom.

The contagion of these groups will not hold against me. I will make them leave because, they know it, they cannot remain if there does not remain this symbol of freedom for which we fought. Europe is a ground of collection and not of exile, as of the imbeciles could tell you in emissions which destroy you so much. They are gadgets for you lobotomiser.

It is necessary to fight against these propaganda which make you believe any stupid thing. Only the order will be able to rectify our great nation. Only the order is able to be the continent most extremely. Nobody wants that we take the floor because they are afraid which we succeed in being the center of the world, which we always were. It is enough!! Let us begin again what is with us!

39

20 January 2013

All the governments claim with any economic conquest of the world. Well it is false, because was the preoccupation with a their presence to the power, they would understand the difficulty in being able to reconcile the truth of the forgery, especially in term of finance and report of the debt which should be an asset of permanent construction.

The revolutions gave to our nation a whole provision to make us a nation of people which preach and cry their entity. Because yes, we know to be proud of our idea to be of human vis-a-vis nature our mother. For some, ecology has just made an appearance. But for us Viking Celtic Gothics, that was always the case and we always made forests our symbol of truth and full conscience. We are not with the mode. We do not need. We are true identities which built a beautiful world where the calm and the light are found behind our menhirs.

Europe must be this passage to the new era which will give again with our tribes the direction even of this vote which characterized since Milena our manner of deciding and to find the ways. Nobody can undertake any conquest in Europe because we are not to sell and our grounds are high in the respect of the supreme era.

Alliances of our grounds will be a revolution with the eyes of the world which will never understand the unit of our body.

We will set out again neither on a triplies nor on a treaty of Versailles of 1919. However, still present at the hour when we speak and even more than ever. It is necessary to finish some with the Napoleonean code which is there only to be used a company as go-getters who were devoted by all these governments loan to very to destroy Europe and to make this discord a personal power.

The hour is not with defense but with the attack and I see legions of women who want to fight for their right to be and not to be too stupid slaves of men who still see in the woman only the weakness whereas we have, as our history, lived under the domination of some of them which showed a face much more aggressive which we need to discover the way which leads to glory victorious people.

The moment came for us to choose and turn into to alliances between us people and tribes of north, to live our destiny and not to hope any more because dreamed does not exist and we must take and overcome to save our Europe and to control our future. Let us not be blind and slaves of the impossible one. Let us not be philosophers on realistic by whom nothing comes except for misery and the forfeiture. It is enough these political dominations which are not used for nothing. Let us shout our outcome of our great nation.

Let us build our ground and let us not listen to these impostors of finance ready with very to gain until the last symbol of the poverty and the slavery of the men who confine us in an erroneous relation of living and to be the tribes which gained the battles and made of this world a ground for all.

40

20 January 2013

A ground for all does not want to say for all the world tribes. This is not without consequences obviously. Our tradition is based on the fact that if you do not engage your life itself, never you will not gain it, your life of course I think of being clear.

The sacrifice of the individual existence is vital to ensure the conservation of the races Viking, Celtic, Gothic and that our Europe after 35,000 years continues to be glorified by our regard. If one day next I can then I want that my dreamed to be plain like the 13 large royal tribes to continue dreamed of a whole life to be protected and of living in this harmony which is ours where happiness and joy gratify us in the hope of a better world.

I would like to see or to know that my people began again with grounds of our territory and to form heroic virtues and to scorn the parasites which convey an equal untrue hypocrisy even they has madden

Let us find our foundations of our great nation and consolidate with our hands cement which makes us these proud people and which never fought without its bagpipes which made our reputation in the middle of the others.

Our people will not be vandalised and condemn by traitors who have as doctrines the perfidious trick of the parasites. The lack of intelligence and the lack of courage hide behind the stupidity of certain human feelings oneself saying to describe this cowardice of the man who should quite simply carry out to want to sell its need. Version of the denouncement which was the print even Second World War and which is the result of men and not of women who, for a bread end, let kill out of the innocent ones.

The force of an interior state cannot claim has economic blooming because never qualities constructors of the states were dependent has the economy but here, still a lie created of any part by its politicians who, the fear, think of giving you the possibility of voting for them and of continuing their swindle while you continue to suffer.

Innumerable examples show us that the decline of a state is close.

And if the formation of the human communities were explained initially by the action of the forces or the economic mobiles, it would be the maximum economic development which should mean the height of power of the State and not the reverse. However, it is not the case.

The belief in the economic force for the foundation or the conservation of a great nation appears especially incomprehensible, when one meets it in a country where the history, with each step, shows the opposite in a clear and repeated way.

In the history, we showed as only morals qualities built a country. They are also the means of preserving a country even in the event of extreme problems due to an interference politico economic vacuum of its cases by quite malevolent people. Creations which support the nation must flower to preserve the voracity of human of living even through the most terrible conflicts.

With each time certain groups tried to make economy the central point of our continent or others, the idealistic virtues blazed up and the state crumbled in a terrible loss and without future. Yes one needs the spirit and the will of sacrifice of each individual for this community and to make wishes of living for this one and only it at the cost of any sacrifice.

The virtues of sacrifice for Europe do not have anything common run with the economy, which comes out from this simple fact that the man never sacrifices himself for this one. I.e. one does not die for a business, but for an ideal and this ideal, it is the great meeting of Europe... And of its tribes.

41

26 January 2013

Men and women of Europe.

The game of Europe will not be done through the statesmen. If full with spirits will be surprised change of mentality!! So much so that they will never understand the men because they have in them only personal economic interests and do not live for our great nation. They make very to avoid death, as much as they can, at any price of course. They are ready to destroy and to take lives because their only goal is to taste with the fruit of the eternal victory written with ink in the books of history.

The woman, heroin of our large Europe, mother, wife of the hearth and our fatherland which, during ages, fights and fights for the conservation of its race and this state which it defends at the cost of her blood. She is in first line in front of the enemies in charge of their doctrines and their statement without base, which wants to destroy the symbol even of the mother and the woman. One would believe oneself in remote regions, in centuries belonging to the lapse of memory and that we, Vikings, Celtic, Gothic us never knew in any event.

Always, one will be able to proclaim our various formulas like truths such as:

Never a state was founded by these oneself saying pacifist and surely not our continent. But they recall me to tell them of a strong voice which I am for the conservation of my race and which they are not welcome. And even as today, we have decides to ask them to start from the full liking or we will be obliged to help them there. Because we will find in the form of regulations our laws which authorize and prohibit not only their worship, but also their hypocrisy and their lies, as all that does not correspond has our waitings according to our Aryan laws.

Heroism is the instinct for self-preservation of the race Viking which answers the work of the culture. Let us not forget that all the parallel economy represents the beginning and the first case of control and oppression and it is the system which the foreigners want to oblige us to adopt...

The faith which one had before the war, this faith in our great nation and not in this masquerade of the religions which try to make populism to recover voices as a vulgar politician whereas everyone knows that all that is false and does not exist. We must have faith of the possibility of conquering the worldwide markets and of monopolizing world by the political and commercial way. What we must have today it is only and simply the force of the will and the decision of the action.

Our political instinct is simple. The only possible explanation is this force and which I had already learned how to know from another point of view and which returns against me like doctrines and a design which can carry out our life has a true organization.

I understood that the destruction which had come out at the time of the History of Europe had influenced the history of our people and had impressed me in the observation of the policy and of the attempts to control this stinking world plague which now tried to corrode our people by so enormous pretenses that it would have was necessary to be an imbecile not to see them and uncover this mediocrity which I had seen very often in countries under developed which bought the concepts with agents often returned for their incompetence...

The rhetoric of the cultural life and economic was to be carried out by a policy in the order. This order was to be written point by point for an exemplary discipline which never frightened our people but indeed the abroad who live in their clean waste and which is delighted in their pessimism at the point to destroy of them the only installations paid by foundations of assistance only made to come to power of the cash economy.

These foreign people are only pleurnichards and are not worthy of living on our premises. We do not want any more. One moment ago when enough is the word which defines an end of a cycle which cannot return any more behind nor to find solutions.

If they believe power to impress us with larval threats... Station with them. Our patience has limits. One day is spirit to come where we will nail the nozzle with these dirty liars. The members of the party TIC can be reassured: the end of the terror from abroad is closer than imagine it to you. Sirs foreigners: wait you to taste like never before! People, rise! Storm, breaks out! You raise and are beings of will.

V

The Second World War and its Lies

42

2 February 2013

How it is difficult for me to begin this chapter. And I have doubts.

How to make for reading between the lines and rendering comprehensible to you what I read and to share it with you?

To visualize and understand the Second World War it is necessary to know and to understand the motivations of certain people who created lies of any part out of fear of a future which, according to these same people, could be much more powerful than any form of never being able still lived.

I was born at one moment when the war was a provocation like that of the Viêt - Nam. The communist groups Russian-Stalinist knew to make pass from the messages to youths of the east to create terrorist groups and to assert themselves of a pure and hard Marxism which was only one trickery. One moreover, come dictators Bolsheviks. After Second World War was terrible and I do not speak about losses but what that could set up. Or in other words, a vulnerable company captive of a free world going in an extremist liberalism to prove an existence created on the debt and the desire of certain groups for destroying Europe forever because of oneself saying badly which corrodes each European of Viking, Gothic and Celtic origin.

The States started to resemble more and more companies which mutually dig the ground under their feet, try to mutually blow the customers and the orders and to injure various ways mutually, putting all that in scene with accompaniment of clamors as noisy as inoffensive.

They tried to make of note world a Grand Bazaar and to control the impossible one to make vulnerable our barriers, our borders.

These borders which are the fruit of our blood and the desire for being free and for choosing what we let us please be, starting by being the human ones knowing to read and write. This border where we had placed ready soldiers has to fight for our freedom and who were destroyed for groups of impostors come to be used for itself in our trunks and of the same destroying our traditions out of fear of a possible rising of the intellectual forces. It is so much simpler to have commanders who do not direct anything and which does not know anything... Not even to carry out an order. How to believe at that time which destroyed our families? How to believe in these people who, the every day, continue to carry their hatred against our people to impoverish us? The war was a dirty history on all the sides and takes another made way of lie and resources well too poor.

I was always astonished to see documents reappearing. Those where the only thing which one can see there is that the people of Europe were monsters whereas the others were only subjected. However, I would want to give the order to all of knowing what domination and tender represent on a psychiatric point of view. It would be even more interesting if one were to judge everyone and especially to characterize by violence. Then why not to go until the section of the road? Why stop whereas it is now that the history starts...?

This company of Balkans will be always a problem. It is well for this reason which Tito had found of the means that nobody knew to disturb and on the contrary even invited to respect the solitarism of this dictator. One would like to know what its family became besides. Balkans were always sources of problems and are it still. What will be necessary it to make to sacrifice its territories or to sacrifice its texts.

43

2 February 2013

I see today this war like a point of History not finished and that I could finally close the day when I will have answered all the questions which sound in my sucks like tests without ends and which make me suffer so much there are not enough precise details at the key time; and there are only assembled scenarios of all parts which destroy any possibility of opposite. Do you know a war where all is white/blue? It is like a divorce where the husband and the woman reproach the wrongs instead of saying that the wrongs are shared and that they are of 50/50... And not 100/0.

Once again, the fault is always shared and that is necessary to the most point.

I do not have either shame to say today that a fight for freedom is committed and is such as the ground had never seen some of more powerful because we had been thorough until deepest of our cuttings off, at the point to make us pay a tribe of which we are not however the torturer nor the victims but which, at the end, gave us the feeling to be slaves of a company which was not ours. And in fact, to be of bad with dimensions of the barrier.

What could be more prestigious than to believe in a cause and to fight for this one? I do not want to blindly believe any more all that one tells me. It is of course and logical. I came so that the people see clearly in its own future. Thus, with the beginning of this gigantic fight, will mingle with the inflamed enthusiasm most serious that the necessary one can even imagine to him.

I am for the popular exaltation and it will not be a fire of straw. Not, surely not! It will be possible no to stop it because precisely, this war has plan our world in a 21th century makes esoteric beliefs, same fruits of our tradition and which is translated at the others in various visions of exorcisms at the point to make us pass for diabolic beings. It should be said that a kilt regiment can frighten, even today.

The war. Isn't this these sentences heard so often by generals and soldiers?: "Sirs. The serious one is only too necessary; one generally has no idea length and possible duration of the fight which starts. One thinks of finding oneself at home for the winter, and of continuing to work peacefully on new bases. But makes of it the history is another which was written between Red Cross, prisoners and punishments of the winner ready with any lowness to leave itself there.

To be able to rebuild the winged falcon and to shout its revenge at all costs on a man who is a soldier and not a pawn on a chess-board. What became these dogs which wanted to kill everyone and it why of this brutality? How can I accept it whereas one asks to be magnanimous? What wants to say all these words and these good intentions if is not to destroy people, whereas it is so easy in these moments to do it and live on a road traced with the compass in a still wet map of the blood of the printing ink, that reflects the feeling of hatred and tender of these impostors, that they are politicians or ordinary citizens out of fear of being bad side instead of affirming their faith and their cause.

What the Viking, Gothic, Celtic man wish – and I say the Man within the meaning of the human one, of course – is to hope and believe to be to guide by a being which can carry out the reins of the grounds of Odin. The majority of the nation cannot live any more like formerly. And yet, it is what it occurs in this growing insecurity. This one even which is indeed perpetual at the point to today see badly high children of foreign countries striking women to steal their good to them and not to punish them as they deserve it in the their cutting hands as that occurs in their own country.

Our ground is a ground of exile for the respect and the defense of freedom to be a Viking. Not to surely let small groups of rots take to us without reacting. Teach them that you did everything to create a new world with the center even of our great nation, but that all this is finished and that the second world war will become an example of war which will have been the combat of the order against impostors who had already believed to be essential for our life.

44

9 February 2013

My proposals are very clear and simple. Our nation must be or not be. Must one continue to be made insult in our truth and our combat. The satisfaction of the man and the warrior is part of our traditions and I do not have an order to receive people which still kept goats 50 years ago and which do not know what the democracy represents, except for contracts of combined and to be able to come to make on our premises what is prohibited on their premises between alcohol, women of easy virtue and more still. The fight of Europe and our people will be even more inflamed. And when they learn the truth, they will be even stronger and the alarm clock will be fatal for impostors and vermin's which they all are. This fight will be carried out victoriously until the end. Then our people will return to take their place in the circle of the great nations by their external power. And then the empire would become again the powerful heaven of peace, without being obliged to frustrate their children of lies of the large swindlers who, since the Russian loan until our days, always have the same face... That in particular of Madoff. For me adolescent, European enthusiasm was not a vain dream. And envies it to shout the nonsenses of the leaders and of the evil which they had made with our nation since more than one century was the egoistic result of my own will to satisfy me to have done everything against this infamy of conspirators who remained unpunished so far. Yes, I wanted to finally make rediscover through Europe of the regions happiness to measure its people worthy of their feelings and which were ready to make oath of their sincerity in front of energies which constituted the kingdom that we must rebuild, by the strength of our blood and of our sweat, to protect this tradition which wanted to live again of its ashes at any price. I cannot be even any more me even in this Europe which destroyed my rights because of a war which was an engine of hatred and destruction since 1945, and the arrival of the armies which, on the passage, caused even more deaths and the innocent ones. It is so easy to judge...

But after war was never judged! Quite to the contrary... And of many criminals were never judged. And even they were incensed. We need the truth. We should know what it really occurred and to stop listening to these historians paid by groups which are there to rot our traditions and our origins. Yes my friends. The world is afraid as of our tribes Viking, Celtic, Gothics because they represent the symbol of the unit and the first political and economic continent. Since the 10th century, we have grow and build a continent rich and ready to consume, to even live in peace with him. The other people were welcome in the ultimate condition which they marry our traditions and which never they can make their traditions – fact nuns – any symbol or which would be signaled to destroy our identity. What wanted to be made during centuries until now. The people of Europe revolted and that is enough. It is the one era end and the moment had unearthed the shield of the peace of our people and had just rebuilt on new bases our unit. The detractors have only with good to be held and will have to prove what they advance with evidence. If not they will be accused for conspiracy as that is the case in the country symbol of the democratic rights. I suffered too much from the second world war and its lies. Certain groups prohibited the hakenkreuz. For which reason? I do not know of it anything and this is a simple example. Of Beat prohibited any regionalistic sign, going until being opposed to the languages such as the Breton one, the Norman one, the Basque, etc... For which reason, if it is not a will to kill our people like made Stalin or Tito with Yugoslavia? When these two watches moved whole populations as of the Fifties... Who said though it is?

45

9 February 2013

I do not want to make speeches on the master key and this war which have ravaged my heart and my thoughts. But I am obliged to denounce these lies created by a propaganda with an aim of destroying our tribes. However, these same people should know that William Wallace said NOT. And that all the tribes gathered with its dimensioned. I am not afraid and I am immortal today. Even if one kills to me, I know that maintaining my legend will be forever present in the hearts of my subjects ready to fight with my with dimensions because they know that I will defend them body and heart to the ultimate breath of life which I will have with this body that Odin gave me while making me human to achieve the goal of my life. I am close to my people and I need neither homages, neither of rights, nor of money and even less gifts.

The only thing to which I am entitled , they are my duties....

It is necessary to take measures against these cheating associations of impostors and robbers come to trample us by sending people ready to evoke any principle. To be able to belong to our company, it would have to be proven to me that these people did all that they could in their own country and to tell me why they are they come, if not to create the disorder and the discord in our nation. I tell you. These people do not have any right here. This is indeed finished. As we do not have the choice, we must evoke the American right and make in the same way. To be American, in the symbol of the democracy, or right to have papers and before touching unspecified money, it is necessary to have worked 10 years or more for the federal state and given of its labor in terms of taxes and of must rax.

The European blue-collar workers must understand that we must weed this oneself saying international solidarity which pushed French writers and European to take sides blindness for Stalin who caused more a large number of death and much more than Germany even if American is given some to heart joy since the Viêt – Nam. And this cold war was surely hardest and unjust that Europe has food against all and without the assistance of anyone. This ambitiousness of intellectuals which are part of organizations created to prevent our claims must disappear because they are not legal and cause the development of structures which wish to come to power and to destroy our civilisation

As long as I will be there, nobody will be able any more to destroy us. I will drive out one by one these non-believers, returning them in their respective countries where the only reception which they will have will be the prison, obviously.

We will walk under the statement of Kant and in the worthy line of Robespierre to take again each stone. That each and everyone knows that we are the Masters of our places and that nobody will explain us how to make to organize or live in our territories. Any person who will propose herself and justify of a right to threaten to us will be accused of conspiracy in front of the Vikings people, Celtic, Gothic and will have to be judged in front of a court of the people for insult to the base of our civilization and will have to pay without handing-over of any consideration.

You awake while the honest tribes dream of their identity. The criminals perjury and organize their revolution known as cultural whereas it is only nun. Any special treatment towards the policies must be canceled and they must be judged like ordinary citizens. It will be out of the question which they profit from any immunity.

The question, my brothers tribes, whom is we do owe? To imprison the leaders immediately? To make pass in judgment and disencumber the nation of it? It is necessary to use all the military forces and police dice now which must themselves join our orders and swear loyalty to their oath of obedience towards the order of the nation to protect and serve his/her brother and to use dice now all the means to exterminate by the forces any stench.

It will be necessary that the parties show in good faith and prove their accounts and that they show that they used of unspecified advantages... What will not be hard to prove considering all the abuses and the evidence that we have already in our possession on the notes of dinners in restaurants reaching the wages of a blue-collar worker. It is necessary that the Parliament follows our directives and finds an identity which corresponds to the true democracy and not with this mediocrity which is currently even. Who of you knows how many deputies has the European assembly??

Are needed regional Parliaments. One needs a true decentralization for a better company which will centralize in the form of federal laws giving to the regions the rights to manage itself.

Let us not forget that the existence of our people and our tribes are concerned.

46

17 February 2013

The people are thorough with protests because of its lies which were assembled of all parts after the war by recovering this infamous treaty of Versailles. The people felt persecuted by these foreign groups speaking about their religions like an irrefutable fact whereas we, people Viking, live in spirituality in agreement with the nature and the respect of this one. It is necessary to be opposed and convince all the partisans while starting with the street until virtuality of the social networks.

Thus, we will increase our potential of victory and will solve the problems whose policies did not see the solutions and will see any none... Because you do not find among incompetents and poor of unspecified potential results. I will not quote you all the lies which I will be able to explain you of course but I will do it with a concrete and current direction. With regard to a problem that we have just lived, in fact food hygiene. That is to say the minister did not know anything and in this case, it is serious because that wants to say that it is unable to assume its station. Either it is knew it and it is a liar; In this case, it is necessary to judge it in front of a revolutionary tribunal and to make it carry out. We need order. The empires which made a fortune before Alexandre the Large one so far were created in the order. Only the order is the power of the solution of the economic policy.

The actual value of the operations was carried out by impostors who took to us hostages since the end of the war, by false philo-sophical designs in the idea of the extermination progressive and radical of all the individuals which could have come to power and to share it in Europe of the regions, symbol of our ideas and our people. One should not forget only for the poor ones which directed us, the success of the intention resides only in the long-term and uniform application of the methods to choke doctrines, etc How not to know that the indignation raised by the tested sufferings will bring to the doctrines of old and new followers to be adhered to it with a stronger stubbornness and a deeper hatred of the lies than they met and who weakened them even destroyed... And even much more, out of fear of reprisals on their families until 1989, and even to bring back to their previous the defectors after the distance of the danger.

The consequence of a given conviction is the key to want to fight for a cause. Isn't there good manner to live than that Ci? Stability must rest on philosophical designs impressed of the order. It is the discharge system of the constant energy and the brutal resolution of only one individual, but at the same time it is in the dependence of the change of the personalities, as well as theirs natural and of their power. The philosophical designs, that they are of nature nuns or policies – often it is difficult to trace a delimitation here – combat less for the destruction, in negative matter, of the contrary ideas, which to manage to impose them, in a positive direction, its clean. Thus its fight is less one defense that an attack. Any attempt to fight a moral system by the material force ends up failing, unless the combat takes the shape of an attack to the profit of a new spiritual position. It is only in the mutual fight between two philosophical designs that the weapon of the brute force, used with obstinacy and in a pitiless way, can bring the decision in favor of the party which it supports. I will define what is the authority of State in the calm and the order. Yes, these two principles which we need to flower a healthy economic policy who lives on her heritage like any other continent in the world. It is necessary that you understand that we must return all these political groups and to judge them in front of courts and theirs to give firm prison sentences.

It is necessary to restore the capital punishment which will show that we are generous Europe but which we are not the door mat that certain people think of us. All the policies want our destruction since the end of the second world war and their support by foreign groups which want our destruction. That you listen to me or not today, the army is henceforth goes from there and there will be no possibility of return. Europe is spirit to recover upright and the people start to understand that one lied to him. It is necessary to remember of what did Napoleon or well-known the Prime Minister Bismarck. They wanted to make and developed a strategy while wanting to understand Europe is by naming it the center of the world because it is in any event and this will not change. After war gave in charge of the countries of the people who are there to kill our people. But you can prevent them as we did during the French revolution.

They will leave straight in front of the judges and these judges will be to vote by you, the people of Europe, which will have to choose and inspire this symbol of our traditions. Let us not forget that after the war, they are the leaders of the republics of Europe which were the slaves with the service of the capitalist and Marxist powers. To look at the middle-class politicians, the distance between the classes will appear as very natural lasting all the time where it will not start to act in a politically unfavorable direction for them. The negation of this truth shows only the impudence and also the stupidity of impostor.

VI

Propaganda

47

24 February 2013

There is no policy today without propaganda and it is during the second world war that it took all its rise besides. It should be known that most active on this subject were the Stalinist Marxists and Maoists first of all by causing tidal waves in their own organizations at the point to decapitate their respective chiefs for the election to be it supreme. Because yes, propaganda starts with the worship. And then, you will tell me that this one started there are thousands of years with the religions which carried out a combat without mercy against the nonpublic powers of the moment and of these personalities often war leaders who saw only opulence and vision of them even. But here... Propaganda was going to join the two udders of our companies: religion and policy. Only one and even causes for the power of only one: "me". Often, you will be able to see that I write and I turn around several points because I do not judge to in no case and makes only reports, certainly worrying, but that morals obliges me to describe. Let us take to the case for example poor boy who was immolated by fire in Tunisia, which created Arab spring; firstly, you will see and understand that the recovery of this event by the press, the policy, the monks and the diplomatic world is indeed a propaganda charged to obtain the power to destroy that which is or this to set up in a position of neutrality. All this represents propaganda and this poor soul was well forgotten by the Machiavellian swindle of this media power which wants to take all and not to give anything.

Caution! Propaganda or at least the true one is an art and it is not so easy to make conceal its adversaries. You have the manner of Stalin: I make assassinate everyone. And that of Goebbels: I kill the fruit, i.e. this one even which makes propaganda if not more than the press. You hear well, like me, that the newspapers do not have any right to make you think what they want. And well they are not deprived any and for the majority, they are good rags for the dirty shopping cart of linen.

If it is true that the Net because many concern, even if one also saw through this network a source of propaganda which has an ultimate goal on which I will return later on. The Internet is indeed a tool which remains completely unknown besides for the middle-class parties. From where problems of those to leave them, to understand the networks of them.

I took the time to reflect and conceive the propaganda of our party and the desire for giving another definition to this word often taken as an enemy whereas it is only that which passes the message of the rallying of a group of authority and manner of designing the company of the 21 th century. It was necessary for me to devote itself today to the reflection and with the practical realization of any propaganda which will be the heart of our unit through the party and will give us the smile when we walk in the street armed with our badges preaching our origins and our identity of propaganda. I realized that it missed the symbol on our premises even consumable such as the tee shift which, at American, had become a true worship of propaganda whereas on our premises was more old-fashioned.

How us, owners of the mode in the world, could we make products of such a lowness? And well it makes some is necessary to eradicate all this from top to bottom world. Indeed, the chief is afraid of that which is strong thus it takes as assistant poor or poor to conduct its campaign, if this same person would want itself to present herself to the same elections as him. But what it does not know, it is that poor or good, the person beside him will be beside him as long as the chief will be the chief. And one does not become the chief by elections but one is born chief, it does not have no doubt there above. Then you will quote me names of people who were in front. But was they the chiefs? In be you sour? And well I will be able to prove share A+B to you which you indeed swallowed the instrument of propaganda and which believed there you.

For example I tell you: "mustard is good". Then taste it to you but you do not ask how it is done or which did it. Here is your error.

You were the instrument of the publicity thus of propaganda.

48

24 February 2013

The instruction of this propaganda is the goal of our great cause and by my own skew the will devous to say which I am in all the transparency and nothing to hide you. On the contrary and with the contrario of the others you will know ego very: what I did, which I am, which are my values and what I want to make. Yes, it is true, I am ready to beat me and yes, I want to look myself in a mirror and to tell me that what I do is for me because I need some. I do not want to think that I did not do it. I hate the words which are not used for nothing and I will do everything to apply the solutions. We will take décisionsdans these conditions ultimate. These people are only scarecrows which can frighten birds but surely not with our nation, proud, which must take again a true propaganda to live and overcome impostor. Each one of you must be part of the chain of propaganda and preach our colors, which they see to the wearing of Alexandria. The order and propaganda are only the manners of emptying vermin our nation and we will help it to leave. We will preach our ideas so strong which it will leave because it will be seen surrounded by a concept which will recall him from where it comes, because all these foreigners come themselves from countries created on the propaganda of only one hief, of only one family.

Do not think that you are too fine to accept this lesson. You point out that when you listen to these fine wordss of philosophers who vousparlent of Africa, they live in 400 square meters with 30000 euros the square meter instead of you to occupy of your next: that which is beside you, that which is close, that one calls and which is of your own family. And especially be honest with you even, not as these villains who are misled in the mediocrity of the one useless.

Propaganda is there to achieve a goal and it is the ultimate means.

The goal is the symbol even of the cause and that Ci is the symbol even of human which is defined and protected by propaganda. I can understand that this one does not like everyone and that sometimes its behavior is not clear in the idea of the general interest. But if it is with the service of this cause and that it has the effect of its goal, then it becomes the engine of the implementation of a road roller which can be good or bad. This only if the cause is it installed in theoretical bases which saw its practical form and not generally accepted ideas for personal projects. Propaganda recalls in particular that one lives for its cause and that one belongs to a whole. This whole is a keen example of extreme oiling of the supremacy which one can touch only with its heart.

One should not judge the point of view of the goal of propaganda because it cannot be held for person in charge even if in certain cases it would owe it. But if I stopped on the cause for purpose, then I would write a philosophical book and it is neither the case, neither the place, nor the moment, whereas we want acts and not promises. Because yes, propaganda is not a residue of promises made by a party which elected in its centre a representative who dares to be called chief and whom I call poor or pins up.

My wish and to eradicate all vermin that I swear myself to crush not after step.

My use of propaganda is clear. I fight for the total independence of my people, so that it has bread for its quite dark future which one wants to leave him. I want to use the term "to give" because that points out the term to me "to give in grazing ground". We are not the slaves of these morons. Obviously, the security which could be exerted in what I call the order, because if I give 10 years of prison firm to a robber of portable or 25 years for sexual assault in the subway, everyone goes the knowledge and one will stop attacking you out of fear of this door which is closed on oneself for one period of time which locks up you without television, without anything, with only its regret. Of course and especially I want to live the propaganda which will revive the honor of our great nation. Today I say it, I will fight to give to our people the justice which it deserves because the good-for-nothings do not deserve anything and no freedom.

We live together in a nation to beat us together and to protect our rights if you want to be individualistic, then live in a desert island without anything and anybody. But if you wish to share the cause, then beat you side of propaganda and raise your head when whoever looks at you. Preach your badge, your badge, your t-shirt which shows that you belong to the nation Viking, Celtic, Gothic and that we are on our premises and that today, it is the war. One should not awake a Viking who sleeps. One did not have to awake the lightning of ODIN.

Our people fight on this planet for their existence and the question of being or of not being has just arisen.

All the considerations of humanity and esthetics are reduced to nothing when its cause is destroyed.

49

3 March 2013

Propaganda is not inevitably an escape from feelings against revolutionists come to destroy the others. What can guide a nation if not the dignity of this one and the victory of the freedom which can become a human weapon which quickly conditions this same concept?

Because propaganda was invited for a long time in a combat between the life and death. It is necessary to know and conscious being that this weapon which is propaganda can be more than terrifying and quite detonating... So much more extremely than one can think it. What propaganda today? In what it did evolve through this world of media and networks? One realized besides how certain groups had known to divert the images to be made elect and destroy the one moment old policies to replace them by others. With which must address propaganda?? With the intellectuals or the mass who is not informed or so much little and whom they consolidate in the received middle-class idea of a made future of debts and appropriations, history to accept in the modern man and this image created of all parts by songs and icons at the time of the processions of the 1ermai, symbol of a propaganda of the happy blue-collar worker in a world of the 21èmesiècle. The intellectuals for a long time made their hobby-horse of propaganda by creating intonations of voice on the plates of televisions and while taking of title of philosophers or professors whereas their wish would be to be dictators in their turn, of Stalin with Mao, who would see himself glorifying and be able to attend the triumph of their death.

But propaganda for a long time became the court of re-creation of the artists dominated by the desire for becoming and for existing, to draw attention that it is on posters or television commercials. The idea that an image can evoke you the history of a film got an increasingly strong desire to destroy the non-existent one and to mean by photographs of the desires for creating yours. Propaganda is not there to mark the images but to report a fact through an image. But from that Ci can be born only one man who leaves water by its presence and its charisma. Vis-a-vis him, these media become the weapon of the stabilization of an economic power which benefits the way from the existentialism from the man. The need for the image and the controversies becomes the call to the feeling ot the reason.

Propaganda is in any event popular and brought by these people which placed it on the level of spirituality which assimilates the policy and the tradition has our people of Europe.

For my part, my manner and my will to speak about propaganda want to be to define the conditions under which I will maintain moral face I will cause a drop in the enemy in front of us. I will throw any emotional consideration with the nettles. The policy, ladies and gentlemen, are not a field of lavender and the nation is not a park of animation such as Astérix or Disney but indeed a combat. We fight for this ground where all those which come on our premises try to conquer us and to imprison us in the meshs of their quite large nets which overflow of all shares. The crowd psychology changed because you were lobotomisé the brain with sentences drawn from the biblical lesson such as "giving the right cheek", etc.

But when are you stolen, whom you want moreover? You to make kill?? Propaganda is there to make share with all the danger and the hypocrisy of these infamous liars who live in their chauffeur-driven car. Here is a man, Giuseppe Piero "Beppe Grillo" who, thanks to propaganda, obtained 25 per hundred of obtainings voice and which condemned the political system and finally had win against this refuse of Mario Monti which will have done everything in its life, of Communism to liberalism.

Propaganda is there to give, has all the sound of a voice which sounded the end and the beginning of new wanders of 1789.

We do not let lead by self saying aesthetes who are has their air of blasé people ready with very to destroy our content of action and to firmly create the expression of a literary living room for goal to create an opinion which would generate a wind of revolt. Who created the revolts? Not mass, but the intellectual medium which 'is revolted against his/her fathers and the aberration of those. But in this case, it is much more serious! We left the orders to the impostors paid by enemies ready with very to destroy us.

No difference must, to in no case, to modify the content of what is the object of propaganda. But it must always, in the final analysis, repeat the same thing. It is what one calls the "hammer therapy" in language of communication.

The watchword can wellness enlightened on various sides, but the goal of any talk must always be reduced to the same formula. It is thus only that propaganda can and must act with spirit of continuation and cohesion.

Propaganda is in the street.
It has a face, mine.
It has a name, Tradition, Identity and Culture.

VII

Revolution

50

13 March 2013

Isn't the revolution the beginning of a new beginning? Isn't it a revival which one needs? In the end of the Seventies, time of the punk movement, one shouted "No future" like a state to be after two explosions of the courses of the oil crude and the lies of the political bunches which set up the dictators like the ayatollah Khomeiny by concern of taking part in the conflict arabo - oil orchestrated by American and Russian or more probably the CIA and the KGB.

The revolution, it is to find the truth not only in the direction even of this revolt which pushes to take up arms and has to found an army which feels in its leader the respect and the report of this one like the axesine qua nonede this idea philosophical to be and to want. As said William Wallace "cry freedom" to the point to put its life, its blood concerned to save this freedom which forms integral part of our structure of the tribes Vikings.

Will and the intention of the revolution resident in its chief who incarnates the values of the revolution to begin again and not to come to power with the swindlers who were misled in vermin within our company to finish some with our good.

The revolution was always a symbol of revolt well before that of 1789, in France nevertheless. Seemingly, what moreover "utopian" and "idealist" that projects of perpetual peace which is born throughout this modern time? ....

The revolution is often devoted by this image which peace must resound in our modern and Western societies whereas this one is seen diverted of its origin to answer ideas of democracies which are seen related to this model. Then here is an interesting theorem which is to have the right to make a revolution if it is made within the framework create a new democracy symbol even of peace. Ah these white doves of Mr Picasso for wild horizons which refuse with the image of a unit a policy linked to sell intentions of order republicains inked in the cheating of the non-believers.

The revolution is for me today the only means that it remains us to leave this mediocrity and to leave the malignant one our nation to carry out the ideals that only the reason can reach: the one day intoxication better because the open way will turn our company only in one wretched control of a power disparaged by the same policies that we have on the Eastern revolutions called Arab spring.

Nature wants to however prevent the man and opposes to him a constraint to resist this revolution which however should manage a civil society which will criticize all points misusing of a power coming from outside and referring to images made to deaden the children but who do not have any more any impact on the intellectual and working world.

Stop seeking has to preserve your personal comfort and to think even has you. You must be plain in the force of the nation and do all for this idea to be the people units. Those which contributed to this ground and which will fight for this nature even more beautiful the every day than we knew to cure and not exploit like any foreign body seeking only this profit. Be together the human ones which is drawn up and not of the paupers who want only the fruit of a bread stale to express an embarrassment and who will give to their future people only the wretched impression of pure selfishness in all its splencour.

The revolution is our only hope and we must throw out of our grounds those which wanted to rot it and return to the state of grace which is asserted in the light. Perpetual peace is not the consequence of a daydream of visionary if it is carried out by a leader who lives for the ideas of our nation and which feels in its blood to run the truth of the Vikings people, Celtic, Gothic.

51

20 March 2013

What is what the revolution wants to say today? And which was its role since Socrate with, if it is only the means of some of taking over the reins of the political apparatus to find there a pleasure to direct and to accept themselves the top of the others, to today exceed even the myths of the gods of them.

The revolution it is a desire for wanting to find itself and for taking the beginning not to be appropriate of an end and for diverting the good and the evil in a political direction in extreme cases of philosophy, history to find the way of saying what one thinks or not. The revolutionary faces were made to fight one against the other and to give the power to poor insects such as Stalin, Hitler, Napoleon and others.

Did you believe only one times that these people wrote what they wrote, that they made what they made? Be serious two seconds and reflect... When you want to create a company, of how much people you need to make the product, to create it, send it, pack it and without forgetting the communication, accounting, the legal one, the customs, the costs of export... In short you see well that these beings were only puppets in the pay of a power much more pernicious.

Yes but then which? Did they change? For this reason a revolution would finally enable us to destroy these unclean groups which are lowness even world and which represents the mediocrity and the hatred and whose daily sport is to fly and conceal all that belongs to you.

You awake and take up arms!! Stop thinking of your small comfort of middle-class blue-collar worker who does not understand anything and which does not want to move its bottom.

The revolution must be! And we all must put to us under the banner of the TIC and position.

The revolution of the TIC is a total revolution created of you all. I engage you has to create committees within your streets, of your companies, to imprison your owners and your trade unions which are not better than this employers; I do not speak about the voices which rise but those which came to power of these unions and which protect their place. The revolution fights in the same direction and see appearing the color of the world and the vision to surprise thanks to this kind of propaganda which must destroy this nonknown as. One needs a complete revolution where everyone must justify of what they gain and of what they pay like taxes. It is necessary the prison for any politician who lied and who is introduced like culprit in front of the people and justice. Because yes, justice is to the people and no president or minister is not entitled to more but than it must be. The revolution, it is to give access to the Parliaments, the garden of the Elysium. No person in Europe has the right to life on the dividends of the state.

Today, the men suffer and continue to accept dreamed of the Christmas presents which do not exist. None of these governments is able like me to bring peace to you and the wealth because I will go until the end of the commitment. And I will fight with American, I will create bridges with China, I will develop our companies and I will condemn all that is not on our premises by exemplary sanctions. The letters of lamentations will not change anything. We need this revolution.

Then take the flag of the TIC, carry high and strong the values which are for the politicians of the gags and made spit to them what they are. But one of fout of the laws on the homosexual marriage. How one wants it is work!! Then what. With your small costume very passed by again of this morning, you will do what except for me to promise the moon. Order is needed. Only an army can overcome its enemies. It is necessary to go to the step. Are you prepared to make you "kiss" by the foreigners and so that the governments suck you all that you have?

You rectify and beat you! Look in front of and say not. Let us create together this great revolution and tokens in prison these impostors to see how they are left there has to eat shit.

I am not vulgar but realistic. You want what. A man who speaks to you with his tripe and who is proud to raise his kilt as a sign of freedom and of protest?? Or a man without faith which makes you sermons as a monk who does not understand anything more and does not see where is the hope to be a nation of warrior who will fight costs for higround.

Live the revolution and the free right to life in this great nation, that of Vercingétorix where freedom it is the right to be a Viking, Celt, Gothic and to beat the crisis which threatens our world and will make run the loss if one does not fight all units to redefine the rules.

Let us be proud of our fatherland. Let us be proud those which died for we and deliver our nation of these impostors and from any abroad who will serve another that us even. Loose and be not shown audacity. A constitution is not the key of a perpetual peace. It should be supported fraternity so that the idea of our people which base themselves on the duties links, finally men of only one hand, towards only one goal.

What is that the reason can be except for that of the philosophers in their armchairs which think for you and the choices of knowing give you what it is necessary to make? It is necessary to in any event organize a state of order and not a legal state which fights on nonapplicable laws, history to leave with those which direct the economy to be able to make scandalous traffics.

Let us fight for the order.
The European order of the areas.

VIII

The Desire to Begin my Political Activity

52

21 March 2013

I was in prison and I wondered why of this imprisonment, considering more than 143 people had been stopped by this American democratic government whereas in fact I was guilty before even being tried.

I thought and for the first time of my life, this same life took finally a direction. Yes I was not any more the slave of a world in which I suffered and I had finally a goal. That to beat me to become that which I was to become. When at a stretch a voice was posed on me and a kind of force gave me which will make ego this invincible being ready to undo some with the impossible one: the US government.

The sentence of all the prisoners was always the same "BOP (office of prison), when he you have the hand above to me, you cannot leave there more". It is true that any person who returned in prison found with judgments which did not make less than 10 years firm and I felt in me a terrible desire for beating me.

I do not know why, but this day or my head was posed on the fresh pane of the bus which was to accompany me by a prison with another framed by 8 armed police officers as if we were in Iraq with handcuffs with the hands with the feet and a chain which surrounded me the size to be attached to the handcuffs of bottom and top and closed not a lock that I was to weigh up with my hands which were bloodied... They were afraid that armed bands from abroad, come to deliver me!

What made me more and more laugh because I really wondered how this image was born in the brain the depressive ones and thus of prosecutors in evil to be at the point to say to all: "did you googlé it? " you saw, it is everywhere, it is a "big star"... Hey yes, my face was in all the credits of information, which made ego a man dangerous to cut down.

Then I was played of this character and I started to recall me of all my ancestors who had been in prison because of competitions between them. What had been causes the loss of our family of many times at the time of these years that I had known through the books and that while studying I understood more and more why of this imprisonment.

I had always avoided the subjects which annoy such as the parallel policy, oil and economies to return in the universe of art and creation and to live on an artistic projection between mode and painting. Then why did I find myself in prison? Why were these governments afraid of me? Why this desire for putting to me in prison at the United States? Not to be likely any to leave alive considering the number of dead prisoners the every day, those which were not part of gangs or of illegal companies which car are protected in this place from imprisonment which is part of their universe.

All these thoughts were set up in my sucks and I started to awake me; yes, all my life I had wanted to die by testing all the possibilities of suicide or provocations. And for the first time I wanted to live and live for a true goal, to beat me and gain. A lunatic force seized me and I felt indestructible, ready to beat me finally for this political idea which was in me since very small, so much so that I remembered of this moment when, at the age of 9 or 10 years, I scarified myself to register a symbol prohibited Viking oneself saying since the war and which for me represented more than the impossible one, the interdict. But which had been able well to prohibit this idiocy and why? Isn't the human one able to make allowances? Is what the democracy can allow to prohibit without being justified?

Here, I returned in policy and maintaining it was known as. I was going to beat me to become what I think. My ancestors would have been proud of me this man who refuses and accepts what must be to be appropriate of a destiny and of a possible one following day futuristic image which promises one day better. Because one fights and one never lets detractors come to fight with its dimensions. I analyzed the policy of Europe and I set up a game to see whether I were able to dominate the prisoners over a subject which they did not know. By knowing that they placed France below Mexico or beside Iran, i.e. for them in Australia. Yes, the geography is not the fort of American and even less of the people in prison, therefore the best guinea-pigs for me. Because if I had been able to dominate them and that my speech touched them to fight for my opinions, then I will manage to gain control of a political system based on the order and projections of a great nation. I had considered the role of Europe and I had understood that Europe was the only continent which was born from its traditions. Role completely differ and in fact has the geopolitical opposite of the systems which could be North America or of the south, Asia or Africa. Yes Europe in 1905 had seen appearing demonstrations of support with the nations created of any part against the system of Europe of the regions. These wills had been supported after the war of 14/18 and had been expressed by the treaty of Versailles of 1919 and had hastened by the same one to create the company of the nations. Yes then my combat would be against this imposture and for the re-establishment of Europe of the regions which represented the future of Europe.

I understood more and more my role in these prisons and in front of these judges and large jury by amusing me and by taking the fold to be able to use all the possibilities to leave this hell whereas the judgments had thrown me in prison for tens of years firm whereas I was in comas due my genetic disease has which touched my brain: the cavernamatosis on epilepsy: DNA of our family. Yes, if I managed to leave this conspiracy then indeed, I would give my life to Viking people to gather at the cost of blood Europe of my grandfathers.

It was necessary that I create a new party which applies the political training of the European circles which were not found any more in the traditional parties which had exhausted the resources so much that they had any more no credibility.

53

24 March 2013

I really decided to launch me in the policy when I saw that the policies were poor people. I thought on the contrary that the policy needed not only great men or of large women but also of exceptional people who had understood that the policy was a priesthood and who did not have anything to gain there, not. Neither money, nor thank you, but a personal satisfaction to say itself "I did it". This was for me most important and necessary in my everyday life. I had a hard time to understand the past of my family and the past of our history considering all the official books of history and policy are false and were written by impostors in the pay of great financial groups which one must destroy. Not to survive but take again the power. The power has only one word: "the order". What I want to do of my political commitment it is me to beat to find solutions which are in front of us and whose politicians do not have any idea, because they are only puppets unable to write their own texts. Of course, I do not speak to work in team. But if the leader Na not of personal convictions nor of outcome of situation then it does not have there possibilities. All the programs are false. I do not see the policy in 60 points but in three points. And if one manages to start the three points, then it is the end of the crisis. I will not speak to you about such or such politician because to speak about this mediocrity it is already a waste of time. Not, I will explain you my desire for beating me on the economic problems which are not and I go can be to surprise you. But you ask the questions rather: why the fall of Europe? For which that is used it? When you have the answers then you will have an overall picture on the world business and why of these problems. The American democracy is the symbol of the world democracy. What does it make when a policy made an error? It goes in prison. What does it make when a trader flies of the money? It goes in prison. And yes, the same law for all. To steal a Mobylette or to create a speculative bottom, to inflate the sales turnovers to resell with highest and to develop within the companies of the insider trading... Here is the diagram that the politicking ones offers to you. There is no more line or of left. All that it is still a made lie so that you fall into the panel and that you believe in these actions in televisions which serve their interest. You revolt and take hostage all these people who are traitors with the nation as your ancestors did it with the French revolution. Trust the traditions and beat you to continue to eat country ham and the hand made foie gras of duck. Do not believe that I do not know corporate names related to the economic activities. But it is not by making the goose which one will change and look at the life together. My horizon widened and continuous to take with you the initiative of the scene and to require accounts of the president and of the deputies. I will come with solutions and I have the teams ready to undo some. I need you all. We will not manage to change nor to become again this large Europe without the support of each stone. You rectify and beat you with me. Come to support our action to finish some with the financial slave system. You, European people, you miss clearness in the design and the appreciation of the economic life and its principles. What the capital if not the fruit of produced work Let us return to the truth and or this fruit and which is it. It is necessary to protect the human activity and to give the importance to the power of a state of which everyone must bring its good to save this notion of the results. I want to live with the service of the state and to prohibit any foreign action to become owner of our goods and to make tremble these same foreigners by the force and the order.

The more we will preach the order and the more we will be respected by all these groups which yesterday wanted to steal us and tomorrow will want our protection as they did with American with the difference it is that we are the neighbors of these people which need us because even their manner of creating finance does not return in their convictions, which poses enormous problems of funds without any possibility of return. We must represent freedom, the military force and the order of the nation.

54

4 April 2013

I should speak about the role of the state in the capital. But in this case, I would return on all that was already said by pseudonym intellectuals of the beginning of the 20th century. How could I describe this political devotion which, at the bottom, was since always like a burning fire with deepest of me, and which I redrew with the sandstone of my life through the creativity and the study of theologies. The fear of my grandparents, I suppose, to see this force in me gave them cold in the back because of being it true that Europe was to concern itself its ashes by this knight who would believe in the values passed to give to the present a future always more extremely. I was diverted of this political way because I was afraid of myself and my actions with the question which resounded in my head of child tormented soul: would this be the good decision for a whole people? How can I be in charge of people in my hands? From where the second question which burned me the lips: how an incompetent often even stunned could arrive from a station of a simple town hall to president of the republic, whereas it was not even able to solve its personal problems of couples... And even less vision in the short or medium term of the debt which it had just built in this small town which had required anything of nobody, except for being able to live and understand the world of tomorrow. Then at a stretch I wondered why I made them if fear, with these merchants of the temple, these policies and industrialists. This was not yet and still the same history and the return to prejudices which made ego the leader of people in rout. And if they were all afraid of me, was not this because I was able to transfer them and show that they were not essential, and even as they blocked the rhythm of a civilisation. I will not take concrete examples to you for the moment but it is true that in any event, I was entirely of agreement with the American legal systems on the anti trust. Of which right a person could be authorized to take a market, especially when this one had been helped by wings of a power. I was thus decided to make control on all and I wanted that the people see and realize finally of this abominable conspiracy. Let us imagine, if you have a billion, why have more? Don't you have any have enough? And well not, for these Sirs who would prefer to ruin countries to lose a game where, at the end, it is them the losers because they are insulated generally so much that they finish between 4 boards which do not often even reflect their wealth. I often saw, because of their respective wives and their lovers who are often the best friends besides. In short to take again an expression with the mode, here me is in the moment when I must take all that with the serious one. Yes, but how to start? And by what? And the worst of all, with which? The left and the right-hand side do not exist. All this is a bunch of stupidities made for the illiterates of less than 6 years. That amounts believing into cubes last values who fought for the power and not for convictions as could do it Robespierre or Che Guevara. Then I strolled at everyone in Europe, then the world, to understand which were the challenges of these policies who said so different from/to each other. Then the truth appeared to me... And if everyone political would run after a power as a projection which did not exist?? Yes in fact, none of them had the tiniest conviction to make its priesthood in this profession of faith which was to be a politician. Of course, when I say "man" I speak within the meaning of the human one. In this case above the two women and men are indeed taken into account. One is well far from the cause and of these people who will die for this image which radiates like a sun without voice. But here, I was in the absolute truth. Everyone gave itself of the policy. The policies did not have anything of it to give you, ground and Kantian existentialism. Yes, I was in front of a metaphor of the world and I was going to change it. But to change, the truth should be rewritten. However, all the lexicons of schools were polluted by lies or very often one even exaggerated to opt for such and such solution. But here, it was decided. From now all the signs, images or other symbols and symbolic systems of the people Viking, Celtic, Gothic would be my personal cause. And yes, I will affirm that I do not love impostors who have for me the names of De Gaulle, Churchill, Stalin and Roosevelt who recreated the abominable one. I.e. the Treaty of Versailles of 1919. And I will make very to find this Europe that I like and that I protect. I would restore the order. Not by the force but by the order and the principles of the traditions. I will make of my life the torch of my identity and I traversed my world to preach our culture. I was so to speak hallucinated and increasingly conscious of the lack of culture and this imprisonment of which we were the slaves by seeing the people asking to me whether I were Scottish, because I carried the kilt, symbol of all the people Viking, Celtic, Gothic. I.e. 17,400 tribes. But worst it is than these same people did not see their lack of culture not to know that Scotland had counted two large tribes: Picts and Scots. Yes, by leaning me on my political vision, I understood the destruction of our culture by a globalisation Maoist, history to think similar. Yes but which wanted that so not the religions which live only in the imposture and the mediocrity of the people and make accept certain elected officials who they will be the new kings or magi through titles resounding of contempt and opportunism. I could not accept any more the contemptible speeches of certain policies such as Holland who had lived only between Robuchon and Lipp. Or Mélenchon go-getters and proud to be it best. But which had for simple reasoning to only make you believe what you want to hear. And as Coluche would have said: "when it is thought that it would be enough that you do not buy any more so that does not sell any more: nevertheless do you exaggerate a little bit, not!!? " A little humour to make pass the pill will say my detractors. I do not need people menaçantes to answer of whom I am and of what I can do and what I will do in any event because my life has one watchword today: my people or death. What was this reality which took us along the world if not in the abysses of nothing? I was at a stretch shock by the racism of all its people in all its remote regions. Amusing to see that Chinese of Singapore to treat me of dirty American by throwing me with the mouth my bag of provision. And which vision of this oneself saying South Africa even more racist than the parties of apartheid but so normal when the human one is dirty. Yes, dirty and disagreeable and like the animals the concept of the territory has which it conquered. All the great causes as the great projects have one goal that to harm the unfolding of the bodies of the world. Yes, ecology. This word which had appeared as a powder trail so that the policies have finally something to say on the plates of televisions. Because I tell you, I at all do not want to tighten the hand with these impostors. I would prefer to cross to them rather than another thing. And I think that its dwarves understood it well. Thus ecology where the reports rained on both sides. Yes but which does what and how? And of ecology, it is well! But to create job thus or how and when?? Or lalalala! But I asked some policies unable too much to create though it is... But me, I had anything of it to make of their answers because I had already found ways to develop the business of ecology. I remember one day when the administration had sent to me a spy hidden behind a beautiful panoply of redundant titles, which spoke about the fishing out dune finery and its pitiful report where they had already decided to close it then qu ' they continued has to turn into to promises with the trade unions too much idiots to believe them or make accept their militants that they had paid a contribution for nothing, without one moment to find the way of developing the refinery **and not of saving employment but of creating some.**

IX

People and Tradition

55

13 April 2013

For me, the people and the tradition had resonances of a power of a truth and even perhaps what I would call the truth. In all the cases, mine. And it is what I thought because I wanted to accept and give a hope this world which had lost the principles of being and to live. All that I saw, they were beings such of the zombies of a film B which were repeated unceasingly that this life was better than the other. Then I wanted to shout and move all these waves to make a better world. A world in which I could see my hope to be my mirror and not the nauseous stink of these people from abroad come to invade my ground and even to burn it.

The duty of a state, of a great nation like ours, is to have a respect for our capital which must be relatively clear and simple. We must keep under control our nation and not fold in front of the services of the enemy who can have any face. You forgot, after the washing of brain that one made you, that this tradition is the symbol of the union of our great nation and our people. Because yes, there exists in us a light which since the paddle of times is protected by Marline, which itself finds its power in the breath of the dragon.

Today, awake and hold up your origins Viking, Celtic, Gothic instead of this clothing of shoddy goods which are made in foreign countries under brands and names which place you in boxes to dominate you. Nobody knows the truth of the second world war. And those which know it conceal it because they are afraid of it. Yes, fear of this truth which hurts.

As I told you, a person cannot move the mountains if the others do not help it. And yes, the sad truth it is that everyone believed in a way which carried sometimes the colors of a camp and sometimes those of the other. But at the end, it was always the same thing and the same sonnet: to find a ground which had invented a past, one present, and even a future. But the odious one was still worse of all that. One was going to make books which were going to invent stories to make you believe that a world had existed, with an only aim of dominating you. Some even, were going to think to take again a power or to reinstall themselves whereas the head had been already cut to them. The tradition is the pride of our continent, because our people were born from this one and will continue to live until blood continues to run in the veins of our family.

It is necessary to support an economy and the right of this blood which runs by giving again with each one the power to decide to go until the end. Because yes, the solution is there in front of us to go further. We raise! Let us not be afraid to hold up our banners, to carry our colors. Let us be proud. We will defy the impossible one and we will throw to the sea the enemies of our civilisation.

56

13 April 2013

Before the journalists or other people do not try to corrupt me, I will try to answer all the questions which could be thorny. Yes, when do I speak about the people, this is in populist remarks? Or simply in the direction of the gathering? And well neither one nor the other.

When I speak about the people, I should rather say the people. Because, as I explained, we are not divided, as opposed to what some could believe, but on the contrary multiplied by creating tribes according to the areas and families. Indeed, our people live through our tradition and this one is indeed alive of each one of us. One cannot give up our grounds. They recall us with each time when one is abroad, we miss our traditions.

I was able henceforth to distinguish fundamentalism from all the causes internationalists which had caused the collapse of Russia and had turned China into ultraliberal.

What I had noticed recently, they were that our people had completely or almost forgotten our traditions and our culture through the books written by our enemies for, after the world 2èmeguerre, to forget all that was made by the ones and the others. Yes because there are much more culprits than it is thought. And it is so much easier to judge those which died and cannot defend oneself! This besides was not a proof of democracy. One saw a eagerness on our culture at the point to prohibit our folklore and our mother tongues to us.

It would be necessary rather today to fall the spots on each part which wishes to take up the challenge to give to his/her children the culture as of these grandfathers.

It is while reflecting still and still that I realized swindles against our tradition. But for you, whom tradition wants to say? It is not only to wear one hat or to cover themselves with a coat... But is to find the essential one which is anchored of each one of us and who goes along our cultural identity. Because it is well of this one about which we speak. This same identity which pushes us to help the close tribe to give him the necessary support to increase its opportunities.

Indeed, the capital plunged us in a fight without end. That of the soft food of the money.

And today, you look at! Do you work for what? To prove what? What can't you even pay you 4 weeks of paid vacations? Then for what this game is used where at the end you are losers, even by complying with the rules... The only goal of the politicians is to take a little more every day, on your back, considering which they never worked or almost. And even they forgot. I remember this actor known to Los Angeles which told me how it had been difficult for him to manage its after success, passing from 10,000 dollars has 1 even more million... "To fall down" to 10,000. He explained me how one is accustomed to the luxury and the easy life. Yes, but here. The life is not easy and all that one presents to you is pure propaganda so that you continue to work and buy the products which you produce to enrich one, five, ten or even 100 people. Those there same which play triple forecast gaining in the magazines such as Forbes which are played of ridiculous by giving a ranking of those which have more billion than the others.

But me I will take the ranking and I will make stop all these people. If I gathered the fortune of these 1000 people, I would solve the problem of the worldwide economy. Here, let us look at our tradition and see together that we are not capitalist besides nor Communists. We are the people, these tribes more the hurdy-gurdies of the world which we beat for a single ideal, that to shout our freedom.

57

17 April 2013

The task in which I wanted to develop my program is not to establish an action but to show that this one is realizable. Yes! One should not any more be concerned with what we will have to do to take again our grounds like one makes before us certain peasants in certain countries. Even if after they were ridiculed by men even more lying than the capitalists themselves. Our tradition is to push our people to decide conditions and not to discuss with why these problems which retain the blooming of our identity. Let us not look at behind any more and condemn any impostor and nobody who would have like drank to ruin to us. We never prohibited anyone in our country and we always protected the weak ones... Provided that those recognize that the truth is ours and only ours. If not we will be obliged to return them to their own tribes which wanted, for the majority, to destroy them.

Our power does not have the borders of 1919 but those of our empire. We conquered the world and we hope well to remake it again. The sleeper did not have to be awaked because this one will develop a hatred without return against all those which will have taken the fruit of our tradition. That which Odin, our father, gave us to do it to bear fruit and not a trade without name for the only principle of growing rich. We are against personal enrichment. We think of our village such as it is described in our novels – of king Arthur in Astérix. We think above all for our people and not for ourselves. Let us be proud and hold up the spades of the revolution which started and which nobody will be able to destroy by the force of our tribes.

Let us not let opportunism slip into the absolute truth of this action. We must act for finally becoming the star of our city so that our poles until regild the movement cannot be destroyed by a third any more.

Our size lies in our accuracy to set up these ideas which characterize our quite clear sight and which will give again the value of employment that you let spin between your fingers because you forgot to be there, present and sincere in front of your fathers. And that you to beat for the cause which is ours... Yours!! Only and the single one, until the sky us falls on the head.

I do not want to be the creator of a movement but only one of the machine components. I wish that we build together the engine of our rebirth, thanks to our spirituality which created the world and the habits of the other people, because contrary to us, they know the fear which we do not know. Therefore we are people of warriors, but also of workers of the ground when it is needed. Our human thought can conceive these truths which come us since more than one thousand of years and which created our tradition.

But I go even further and I am not afraid to say it! Those which think that we are fanatic are foreigners who do not even comply with our laws. It is themselves which came, not to live in freedom on our premises but to impose their laws to us. I repeat it to you! It is not question!

It is now the moment for us, warriors of the people, to take again the armed struggle if appreciated by these politicians of right-hand side or left in the Arab countries. And well you will be content Sirs! It is not a spring that I will give you but a true change without flashback. It will be a means of rendering comprehensible to you which we are and which never again you will be able to take of the decisions without us. The truth will burst and I will be there to put to you in a pretty room, in a pretty house, which we call prison and which you will call your home.

X

The First Period of Development

58

29 April 2013

That to say in this first volume, except for speaking about what has occurred for 50 years and presenting to me to you with all the humility of a man whom one has drag in mud by many occasions. Do I have to describe the development of our movement? That which I hope for. That which must draw with deep of our beings. A relief to gather us to save this ground which Odin entrusted to us.

The druids warned us besides while resting on the powerful Marline that this ground was entrusted to us to protect it from that which would make him evil.

I am this sensitive being in front of you who hopes to be joined by you, million women and men, who will be the followers of a different company.

Wishes with deepest of us: to be impatient to shout our will to be to blow and vibrate under the slapping of the standards of our ancestors, pushing the hope of this expression which will lead us to the victory.

What I feel today, after the last large gatherings with the call of a referendum, it is that million living beings in France has, at the bottom of them same, the will of a radical change for better living conditions. Not that which want to do to us to believe these poor politicians who forgot the pain of this way the every day between bus, tram and subway. Not to live but right to survive.

I see in these people de Gaulle of the discouragement and the dislike. Because at the bottom of ourselves the anger of this hidden evil thunders which is indignation. As this furious desire to continue the combat which will not make any more you total abstainers at the time as of elections but, on the contrary, of the resistant volunteers for a world against fanaticism whatever it is. But especially against those which make very to just turn us into ridiculous because we like our menhirs and the legend of king Arthur. We like the love affair and the nudity which is for us a manner of living since the paddle of times. And do we have to change and accept the habits of the others? For what to make? To please foreigners who spit on our traditions and who rise against our operation while benefitting from its advantages?

Our movement is young because it has just been recorded. But it is not it because we are there for a long time... And when I say a long time, I should say since the paddle of times. Some speak about traces Vikings going back to 17,000 years. And recently, NASA claimed to prove our existence 35,000 years ago!! Yes it is obvious! We are the oldest people of the world and we created the languages, the traditions and a culture legendary because we were the first to be written and with reading.

How can one claim to make of our people a nation gathered if we do not have an order.

Yes, we are an army whose fire and water are our commanders. We must respect the order and enforce this order the abroads. I do not have anything against the foreigners. They can come, us always protected them from their own tribes which wanted to very often assassinate them by nonrespect of a law. But to in no case they cannot have our grounds or even order and even to direct. The Vikings laws are strict and it is out of questions which I return above. The laws are not made to change but become better in our daily needs and, as the king said it: *"only if that brings any to me importance"*.

59

1 Mai 2013

Our organization must gather all the nonsatisfied trends. Happy, we are to be to us awaked and to have understood that there is not on our premises right line or of left. That made long time that the United States understood it. And therefore the difference on their premises does not exist.

I want to be the man who takes the floor in the order and whom the police and military authorities put on our side to do only one with the farmers and the blue-collar workers.

I do not want to represent a populism for the simple fact that I would like voices to beat tired others. What interests to me is that we, power of Europe, we take our place in the world and that we stop making problems where it does not have there. I wish that we create genuine platforms of construction for a solution where we would be the dominant ones.

And yes, there are no world without anybody who directs and others which carry out. The world without suffering does not exist. But I cannot be the easy conflict which exists in the whole world and which lives with less than one euro per week.

We are not divided people. We have policies who play division to destroy us, us to crush. Today, each layer of the company has an intellectual level which enables him to react and fight against the ignominy and the silly things of these people who waste their time on plates TVS, where we have the feeling that they discuss together like good long-standing friends.

I tell you, our interest is the nation. And this great nation of Vikings who have creates this large Europe of north to south, of the west in east. We were at the end of the worlds. And while passing, we dominated. Then we understood that our ground recalled us and asked us to return to protect it, to cover it with our hands and our hot hearts.

I use the weapons of spirituality to achieve my objectives. Not because I am obliged, but because it is really my manner of coping with the adversary which receives my determination like a brutality, increasing its sense of inferiority.

I put myself a question. Do I have to accept humiliations of these groups known as political which praise themselves to direct our world without assent of our share and which cloister themselves in silence? Whether it is Sarkozy or Holland... But the others are not better! From Spain in England via Germany.

I am sometimes taken of fear to know more how we will leave. Not of this economic crisis but of this political crisis. Because the knowledge is needed, if you want to leave the crisis, it is necessary to look at the truth opposite and to give the order. But not only in the street, not. In the organizations of state also and to return before the court all the public people of the policy who handled the actions not to be marked. I know that the politicians of all the parties will not have of cease to say evil of me to you and I will make very to tell you the truth on me and them of course. I will tell you all.

60

1 Mai 2013

The social networks are not only the means to develop a true political reaction. We need an action much stronger with a structure than we can animate 24 hours a day/7 days a week. A Web radio operator, new structure between radio and television, where we will be able to give new policy and journalistic good stronger than the magazines of which you had the echoes during years.

If we want to rebuild our European political force, it is necessary to give us means with this need to beat us until the end, never not to fall and continue the fight for the order. Yes, that there mêmequi will make our great nation an unattackable force and extremely well trained not to fall into the nihilism. Yes, I believe in the cleansing of the world Viking by our values and our traditions, words stolen by all the political authorities. Because the groups know that we are spirit to take again the power in pies the forms that considers. Our political conservation will prepare the handing-over in question of all the values of the state to find the chief who will size up in its arms the people which want to become again the capacity of resistance towards the people which threaten us out of fear of our power. It will restructure the cohesion of our determination never to be stopped. And in the accumulation of the visible existence, of the burning will which shows the courage of our cultural identity until in the death and the pleasure of Walhalla.

Our weapon, it is our blood and it is the will to go until the end. They is all our brothers who will fight for becoming it of our desire of a government which answers the people of Europe. I am ready to sacrifice my life for this ground which saw me laughing and crying, which saw me playing, to grow. This ground in which I opened my veins to see running the blood of a family which for more than thousand years has warred north to south and whose members were regarded by its enemies as the largest knights of the Holy Lands.

Our will to live master key by the restoration of our political Viking and the power of our families for the order and the respect of that Ci. Who since the knighthood and the tales of yesteryear fascinated the masses of the people of Europe which rented allegiance has the empire. Our fight will be without mercy and we would reconquer our people which lost the faith. They will find the smile with the truth of our faith of the size of the symbols of our teaching; even if republics 3rd, the 4th or the 5th desired to make us disappear by giving again with our enemies the power. Our blood runs like our rivers and we are puncture-proof.

Look at, it does not have there resistance, it does not have nobody there. Of what are afraid you? Small foreigners flying of the mobile phones in the RER?!? Then you rectify and beat reprocesses them as the police does not have any more the right to make. Let us recreate the police Viking, that which has the right to correct, to protect under the honor, these same which cannot any more, do not want more, so much they are overpowered of a work destroyed by prosecutors who,

I already told you, should be elected by the people with free elections. They are policies like this Minister for the justice which prevented the police from making her trade... But let us recall from where it comes and which it supports. Why continue this policy from abroad? We do not want that these foreigners have unspecified political powers. Even less those coming from islands as the Antilles with which we lose money.

61

28 May 2013

Our development will be done thanks to our institutions and by the respect of those. We will give again a true army and duties with all the citizens to live in agreement with the support of our nation. The alliance of the administrative bodies will be done by political police chiefs who will be there to accompany the unit by the citizens who will have to live for the great nation and not to live for themselves while believing to find in the lies of the extremist liberalism who gives you like proof the existence of the impossible one.

We had many balls which we supported. Today, it is not any more questions. It is necessary to give again in the State the symbol of our chivalrous forces by the solutions of our traditions which carry out us to beat us against the political treason of all these members who betrayed our country and our entity. You must understand that these people who betrayed your confidence and our European entity are the same ones which is allowed to teach us lessons while holding up words and laws. _in addition without your agreement... This idiot of Holland be even not able to choose between two woman nor to come the power with socialist party during 11 year and of know what himself be pass in the bottom monetary of its own party. There are two possibilities: or it is an imbecile, or it is a liar. In both cases, it will release. But it is not worse than Sarkozy or the others. We point out this infamous Giscard...

I want to try to write the various political segments to carry out by our movement for Europe. The spirit of our doctrines passes by the order and the way to respect it. Look at what it occurs with circulation, for example. You do not respect any more fires but the police does not respect any more its work which is to be useful and protect and not to put PV to any person who parks herself badly. But on the other hand to protect the citizens and to enforce the order to them. How to make when are there no chiefs? Because what our people want, it is a chief and a discipline. Look at all these foreigners who do not respect anything! Those which do not find opposite them the same force which frightened them in their own country.

It is necessary to render comprehensible with our people which never left our Europe that these foreigners have of very bad concepts and which all that they want to make is to destroy our company to do theirs of it. It is not new. In fact wars last between us since hundreds of years. The problem is that we lived in a false peace by letting these same people burst in the brook and that today they arrive with not of the requests but of the orders and that politicians as Sarkozy are carried out. I want of it for proof that this Mister is assembling a monetary bottom with the qatari with which it allocated the right not to pay taxes in France.

Our program could be exposed in 60 points like the others and make a volume which you would not read... But it is much simpler than all that! It is necessary made move the system and that all we answer a mechanics which is started like an engine of Rolls Royce and which we went from only one and even not.

To share our ideal which is neither more nor less to continue to live under our traditions.

Let us not forget that we were always the people which respected the traditions of the other tribes, insofar as those also respect us. If one of it attacks us, then we must close the tradition of Odin and ask Thor to close the door with its hammer. In other words, we must cancel straight to whoever, like made American since tens of years. The best example is the Patriot Act, who concluded with a total closure. We must also immediately vote and order.

62

12 June 2013

Yes, more and more I understand that the two things which we miss in all our large Europe are: the order and a chief. Yes the man needs order and I see that the order must be installed from the top of the magistrature until the bottom of the social scale. This one will respect it only if she sees a chief who directs and makes decisions.

We must as of now deciding and ordering. There is one I of foustism in France and Europe which exceeds the understanding. But it is not the entire people which must follow the same goal. And this one is not to be a small middle-class man but to be part of a unit or the independantism does not exist. Those which do not want to fight for the nation do not have anything to make in our company and must start from this ground. It is for that even besides that I give a progress report on laicism. And the fact that all the religions must disappear in the state and the assistances which the state will be able to give. Other shares, it is out of the question to build religious symbols whatever they are. We must prohibit any religious sign in our laic company. Language should be banished any interpretation or report with God or book saying is written by this famous God. I do not prohibit that people can believe in their nonsenses, but only on their premises. I prohibit any propaganda of the religions and any religious sign must be condemned by prison sentences going until the end. I remember to film *The Visitors*.

At one moment, the count asks what our company made with the robbers. And of course it is out of him and leaves a counterpart something the style: "but if the hand is not cut to them, it starts again". Hey yes, indeed, this soft government of the knee of Holland will perish because only the order east does not fear threatening them. I think that the foreigners did not understand. We do not want theirs culture because we must protect our heritage: our traditions. Let us be honest. A warlike woman Viking attracts the glance whereas a buckled poor woman gives desire for crying. Moreover, under their veil, I find that they make dirty and then they are dirty. It is well-known which these people do not wash. And they are the Vikings who invented the soap. There is so much to say, tell, write and share!!!

But the world scandalizes me and I imagine my cousins in full French province and incomprehension that Muslims can take our goods. Once again, and won't I cease repeating it, why these people will not fight at them? The answer is easy because over there, it is hard. And yes, there is not same laxism. I met little time ago, a Maghrebian extraordinary woman like one says. She suffered from the tyranny of the man and the religion. Today it gleams and does not need to have the least not forced. It is this person who is the symbol of a revival of Africa. If one day Africa leaves itself there, it will be thanks to its wives. Exceptions should not be made. The law is the same one for all. My friends, engage – you beside the TIC, because our party is the only one which will be there tomorrow. All the policies have pans with the bottom like one says. Me, everyone knows my course and I am not ashamed of nothing. I do not have any lesson to receive whoever. Then which that you are, come to see me and dialogue with me instead of you to hide via false names on Internet. The truth, it is that only the man exists. There is no God. There is no hell. There is one paradise and it is that which we have here, on ground. We are spirit to destroy it because of anybody who understand only blood.

63

13 June 2013

Of course, you will tell me that I am extremist. Why? Because I extremely say what does everyone low think?? Not, when I am with Barbs in Paris, I do not want to see Marrakech. And not, I do not want to see African who believes that they have a district. Here on this ground Viking, we believe in the tables of our ancestors and only nature is stronger than all. Nature will destroy the infamous one to save our ground. We do not need more than money. We do not need you. We were the nicest people to accommodate you because we believe in the peace of a world between water and fire. We point out our teaching. Among these stories, that of Marline which led us to make an Europe a ground to reconcile and an Western Europe when only we reigned on the world and that other tribes, disappeared today because too proud to believe that they would be there for always, did not do any effort to fight in the dignity of theirs.

The situation is that our initial height is a decisive importance because we believe in the ground. This same ground which gives us the fruit of this food which sets us ablaze in splendour that our empire covered.

Our phase of development cannot be made without you because we all must be plain in front of the nation. Moreover, the chief or that who will be the leader will have to be married with the nation only. The policy is not a game and I would like, with my manner, to show that one can gain as we proved Italy with Beppe Grillo. What one needs is to be together, to fight side by side. There is an enormous building site to set up and will do we it only in the order.

I do not want to be negative and speak about this Empire which collapsed even if it would be interesting to know why and to take stock. How can one speak about Nicolas Sarkozy who belongs to the dustbins of the History? I will be amused to be worried on my book which I write because he preaches a democracy to say and do what one wants since that their serf personally. For me, this effect on our great Empire shows the fall and current weakening.

Already the foundation of these republics is in any event scandalous, as if we were in Las Vegas and in the manner of magicians to gild the pill, using a sleight of hand. Where are the victories that everyone has waited for more 50 years? After May 68 which was to be so incredible, the so brilliant one so that at the end, the reward is the same one as usually: nothing. This is well the opposite of this immortal realism of an economic and political revolution.

Thanks to the order, we will be able to purge all this family of swindlers and unfortunately, even if some are good people, they cannot remain considering it is all the group which one must return to set out again to zero.

64

12 October 2013

It is extreme important to understand today that we are only the survivor of a world in perdition. It is unacceptable to see any foreigner having a ground which does not belong to us because it is beyond the terrestrial property. She belongs to the traditions Viking, Celtic, Gothic. I will make an important point because often I realize that one confuses tribe VIKA – Viking with the era Viking. Indeed, the Vika tribe – Viking is neither more nor less than the elected family. That which has this power to ennoble by reward and to play the political role, legal and economic. Many legends and stories were written on this tribe called sometimes Aryan or chosen people and even descendant of Odin.

The important thing is not in the legend or the history but in the symbol which this family represented and continues to represent today. Even if one deprives it of its rights, it remains a problem for the political and economic leaders who know that only this one can oust them power.

I am the downward one. I am the incarnation of the power I am that which as the volcano will give again has our grounds happiness passes and will drive out never has the intruders.

We must change the face of Europe completely and destroy any opposition whatever it is to find a virgin and healthy land.

We cannot make any compromise, us the most accessible people and most tolerant. We cannot accept any more foreigners who do not comply with our rules and go even until banishing our ground to make their ground of it.

The war is well started and it started a long ago. One day of the year 1974, to be precise. It concretized on September 11th, 2001 by declaring the world war.

Only, if you do not want to see it, you will perish in blood and the fire which these enemy legions made profitable by creating roads of any share to generate the combat.

The policies lie you. Unemployment can be regulated in less than two weeks, as well as the holes of the debt which can be refunded within the same times. The taxes can be retained directly with the source, based on a personal imposition with 21 per hundred and 8 per hundred on the companies. These companies will not have any evil consequently to employ in our grounds and not abroad.

I need the military forces, police and I want to give them a role which is expensive to them: that to protect and serve the tribes of our people. It is completely unthinkable to cancel part of the army. It is necessary to seize all the goods from abroad who will not have legal declarations and to make use of it to build prisons as well as detention centres, as I learned at the time of my visit in the United States.

These years in prison enabled me to understand which wanted to kill me and cut down me so that never again a blue blood of the world Viking reigns on this ground which the dragon protects. But the force, our force, is beyond what they can control. I am here to begin again what has us. I want to see a proud and large army which has the honor of its people. I want to see a police which grows and which inspires young people to be part of it, to devote itself to the cause. Yes, we must fight and live for the cause and only for this one. I would die rather than to see my ground rotted by the enemy.

65

12 October 2013

For our rise, I need each one of you because our freedom depends on it. Our people are rich of their number. Our people have the values of the men and the women. Warlike woman or housewife, who imports, because the woman must have all her freedom because this is a principle since the 8th century on our premises Vikings people, Celtic and Gothics. The honor of the people is seen in this army which fights for its freedoms and maintains its walls which make us people the irreducible ones which never will not take unspecified religion like guide.

The fall of our empire is of our fault. We believed in the messages of the traitors who were sold for money. It is necessary to stop excusing themselves and accepting the finer feelings. How I told you, we are in war! And, as in the Thirties, we are in the same economic and political difficulties. Whereas must we to make to remember us our size and our European past which must flower in an empire of the areas where each one will be able to continue to live according to its historical culture, its traditions and this linguistic identity lost because of these impostors who sold to us.

You awake! Look at all these foreigners who came to eat us, to steal us, to remove us our rights. The traditions are so much forgotten that the children do not know anything any more. They learn at the school from the stories created from all parts by the slide shows come with an aim of crushing us and of destroying us.

I do not want to see any more of coward in front of me in our rows. I want only one and even head which looks in front of and which constrained with that which is not at its place to leave. We do not have another choice only to draw a feature on the past and to set out again to zero. It is out of questions of mingling the policy with all that. All the parties are same blood that of imposture and nonright.

It is necessary to create a militia which will have an authority in agreement with the army and the police to give way to a directory which will set up the necessary reforms which will change our country into 2 weeks. Yes I ask you for two weeks to change our country and to find courage, honor and victory.

One cannot cure of a disease if one does not remove this cancer which corrodes us and which one does not lavish of the drugs to destroy it and set out again with a new skin. It is necessary to operate and cut all this past which draws us behind. Internet created groups of opinions and people without names and faces which speak and insult our values and even trail us in mud by using, like always, the racist images and anti-semites who corrode them so much whereas those want to plunge us in a war since years.

Which teaching draw from this collapse? You try to continue whereas strike while the iron is hot and to change. Not, you are afraid. However the fear kills the spirit. Yes you are afraid of all and to more be able to have your small daily newspaper which however resembles nothing. Made credit and taxes or one promises an equity of rights and knowledge to you in made treat you like machines.

You do not need more evidence. It is necessary to go back to the attack and to rise against impostors and to on our premises drive out them for always. Not by banishing them but in their frightening because they see only the interest. They think only of the power. We must kill the vermin which piled up on our premises. What you see with the Romanian ones exists since De Gaulle: all the foreigners whom France accepted.

The foreigners cannot have the same rights that we and they cannot pay the same taxes. They cannot receive assistances, whether it is unemployment or the family benefits. The foreigners do not have any right in France and we must be regulated on the American democracy with regard to immigration as well as the laws of these laws.

66

21 October 2013

Today, one should not, like each and everyone, to deny which is our cause. Yes, this one even which makes us combatants for the light. The economic distress is not that an excuse of the true cause which reflects the fact of being able to breathe and suffocate in the urgency and to come to the solution which is to take again my kingdom.

The thought of Heidegger is not all and it is it which will lead me to the victory neither even to this decision to beat me but indeed the provocation from abroad who do not respect my culture nor my authority. It 'was never question which you can imagine to be French or European because you are only impure blood, obliged to hang to you to a religion of misery to identify you because nothing in you constitutes some interest.

If the human thought can conceive truths, it is not therefore a clear goal. However given with being accomplished it can be on the contrary an insufficiency of the state of this same being which, by itself, is a corrupted thought.

The truth is that we are in the dead end and that the development of our movement must be clear and not to make an action near partners who meet of nothing the needs for this kingdom. The realization will be made with or without me and this book will be indestructible. It will represent the literary guide of the absolute conviction that we are the tribes of formerly which must live and be. To fight the malignant one which hides behind the invention even of the man and his attributes: religions and their prophets.

These prophets who were often born in the lust and perversion, the fraud and the lie, which have of prophet only the name. But they are frightening politicians in evil to be liked by their own mother often impure in our eyes of Vikings.

The interpretation of the second world war and the structure of its institutions condemned the wheels of an oiled unit which is used today by these same nations which revoked it.

There is no God. There is no creator but a Big Bang which the man in his madness and his dependence reflects to carry out the impossible one at the cost of the life of the man and his entrails. With beyond does not exist and the truth should well be looked at opposite. These people live in the mediocrity to think that can exist a paradise, as the children can imagine a world filled with toys without schools. I tell you. The human one is also low and weak that a 3 year old child and all his fights, it always does not have anything understood and it is by this fact that it must die because it does not represent anything for humanity. Its life imports little. It is nothing and does not have to live because it does not deserve it to in no case.

The religions and their founders are only of cheap entrepreneurs who wanted only to sit their dynasty and to make people of the poor wretches without conviction and nobility. A tribe which would have in fact a goal: that to die for an unknown, invisible and abstract pseudonym creative.

Their ethics does not exist. They are only of vulgar impostors. There once again, I see only beggars able to steal our wheat, which runs in our veins of warlike people. Yes, let us push back together and destroy for always these impostors, these enemies of reality. Let us deprive of their rights. Let us oblige them to leave, in which case we will be obliged to kill them in their actions and to realize dreamed to them to go to the paradise. As my grandfather said, one never should destroy dreamed of a child.

67

2 November 2013

The result of the new taxes is the proof of the incompetence of all the governments which followed one another and the fact that the human one accepts all, the point to pay more for all its foreigners who come to take our ground to us and who do not have any right. To pay for these policies who live with the top of their means. Or not to have the ability more to mobilize and shout the change radical.

I will repeat it once again. It is out of the question to give a penny to unspecified religion. To create a religious identity, it is necessary to prohibit any religion on our ground. The churches and the cathedrals are part of our Gothic cultural heritage and are not a religious symbol. Catholicism in addition is represented by the Vatican which is before a whole laic state. Let us not forget that the papal states represent a third of Italy.

You want the change. But are you ready to beat you? To decide to arrange you under the TIC? It is not any more the hour for elections but for the takeover. The TIC must restructure the army and the police. The goal is to redirect our country of an iron hand, without compassion and in the single will to give to our nations the breath which is owe them.

Is your desire as large as your will to beat you at my sides? Is this the fruit of a true will to come to power to arrange you in a nation without unemployment and which lives for its faith?

Your dissatisfaction is only one additional proof of the collective discouragement and the despair of the whole of the company. But what should rather give you desire for fighting, it is your dislike and the anger which makes indignant your directions. We on television listen to only liars directed by groups which represent these communities which are afraid of us and of our power because they know that this time, we will not hide any more and we will not be afraid any more of these false rumours of which they are the first instigators.

68

2 November 2013

The anger of Brittany is an anger of all our areas. It is necessary to raise our army which only waits to come to power for this furious desire to intervene. The indifference of the policies and the fanatics of the far left go hand in hand to flirt with the youth organizations foreigners of which the goal to destabilize our areas and to steal us our grounds. The intellectual layers of the nation are directed by these groups which are against us. And yet, we are most numerous. But which represents us today? Yes which? Who speaks about our institutions? I want to vomit when I see these documentaries on self saying suburbs where the police is afraid to go... Not only I am not afraid but I will create a militia to restructure the suburbs and to make work any person without employment or under insurance unemployment, RSA for the profit of the community and not for the profit of oneself. We live for a ground and not for oneself. We forgot who we are. We forgot to beat us. It is necessary to take the pulse of the world. We received false information on the last world war. Of course not all because to hide the truth it is necessary to make use and sit an untruth of it to make pass from the ideas. Moreover, did one forget the Stalinist Communists to give as much impact to extremists of left (than I will not name because don't I want any in this guide to make them publicity)? But that I will hasten to denounce on the plates of television where I will be invited progressively. We will control the mediae and those same which control us today. It is not possible any more to quote Dassault or Rothschild like French large families. Disguised impostors, converted by the influence of the power and the money. That points out Carlos Menem to me, Muslim converting with Catholicism to be a president d' Argentine. Consequently, one sees at which point they are ready with very to come to power, since it is necessary to denouncing their traditions. And well me, not. And I want to fight against these impostors who can be only robbers and thus must be condemned. We must seize to them their goods, all their goods in the world for swindle against the state and conspiracy against the nation with the goal of personal enrichment and money laundering.

The ruling class does not have to be able any more and does not have anything any more to make on our premises. It is protected by a very fine fabric which is represented by the police and the army. Those even as the policies disseminated out of fear of these institutions and of the takeover which is profiled. Takeover which must be radical and must send all these impostors in imprisonment for one duration of more than 25 years. To condemn all the children and the families for conspiracy against the nation, with removal of all the goods in all the states where they were to hide their money or monetary instruments. These principles must be retroactive.

A person who stole the state in the Fifties must be judged, condemned then sent in prison without restriction and pity. Justice is there to return the law to all people who made an offence; That it is a president, a minister or a false unemployed user of the social system.

I hate cowardice and yet it is what we became. Lastly, my friends! Let us raise our handles and show our faith. The workers do not have another choice to follow us because these policies are very safe creators of employment and never were it. Look at how the foreigners come on our premises to invade us as if our ground belonged to them!! It is the moment to rise is to shout high and strong our desire of change and dislike.

To reconstitute our political and military force is not any more one question but a fast duty to give again with our entity and our identity a concept of victorious and dangerous people which pose the weapons of supposed the adversaries, which are not mistaken any more while coming on our grounds. Either they come to guarantee their goods because they are afraid of their own people, or because they want to fight against us at the point to destroy us without questions while sending of the military monks ready with very to seize a power which in any event is theirs. From where mediocrity, once again, of these speakers without brain who are themselves of impostors or opportunist system. What in any event returns to same for the history which is in hand.

69

4 November 2013

Our federation must be armed and prepared with the attack of the invaders who came with an aim of destroying us. I know well what certain people say. But in any time and any man dozes revenge and the desire for destroying. Whereas on the contrary, on our premises, the will lives to build a made world of stone and fire. Which is our capacity of resistant? It is worthless because we do not want to suffer any more. Our policies are so much far from us that they are not aware any more of reality and the world which surrounds them. And why? Because they are higher, worthy beings wanting to be to be decapitated by the court of the public hello. The burning will of the conversation of our heritage vis-a-vis policies which, in the right good of the republic and its principles, are able to lower their breeches and are not worthy to control nor to even exist. We must raise our people, with the assistance of the institutions such as the police and the gendarmerie which themselves are threatened, in order to refuse this lifestyle and to make the choice to fight with our with dimensions to protect their family.

Our federal nation will live thanks to men who will link themselves. Alive agreement for the life of a flag which must be planted in all the adverse people and bathe of their blood to show with the others that these grounds are ours and that we prefer to die for this one rather than to see them invaded by this enemy who always envied us because too covetous and conceited to create though it is with its own wealths.

Our people want to fight until the victory. That which will crush the evil and will go until the end, without return, no, and which could not be diverted of its way before the total evacuation of any being which will not return in the constitution written and carried out by this same guideline.

What do we want? To live, isn't? To live to follow our commitment, our cultural identity for this tradition to eat pig (amongst other things). Not with any foreign culture. Yes, I tell you, it is necessary to prohibit any foreign culture and any religion which will not have grown within our culture. There is no question or of answer. There are no laws or of discussion.

It is non final which I preach well high and well extremely. And I tell you: I am happy to eat pig and power food through my culinary culture. I want to drink and sing, because thus is my people. People of brave men and warriors who gave me the ground of their ancestors. How much time, through this hundred years, the infidel tried to colonize us? And how much time did he perish? We threw it beyond the seas, leaving it for dead but, by pity, we left him the women and the children.

We would never have had, because our ancestors would not have done it. And they same will not do it. They are ready to kill their own brother, their own son. Then you imagine... You are anything else only miserable earthworms for these foreigners who want neither to work, nor nothing to make except for taking our place and laughing us with the nose.

70

8 November 2013

The release of our great nation or our federation, call it as you want it, will have to be the idea even of the mass media carrying high and strong our convictions to release forever our grounds of impostors and abroad who do not respect the order.

We will have surely refractories with the fact that we have freedom to think in one oneself saying democracy persuaded by a social populism which will have created only one degradation of the state in him even for a chauvinism with any test.

What to say these pseudonym journalists who have only the map of press and is provided in the luxury to dare to speak about freedom and social vision? The left was always an idea small middle-class men in evil to be and find an assertion against the father - or a certain paternalism should I say - because some could take with the letter my statement.

Our democracy, if there is one of them, starts with the transparency of the accounts but as with a welded and linked army and the respect as one owes him. Indeed, one becomes soldier by conviction to fight and to die on this wall which is the rampart of the freedom and to defend costs which the concept even of the modern society costs which refuses any religious or political fanaticism.

Today like yesterday, doesn't t -it have Judas there of each one of us? What it is Cahuzac or Sarkozy, isn't they all of impostors ready to mow you for 10 pennies?

The brains are not enough and the fists will be necessary to crush the non-believers like made other policies formerly. It is necessary to go on these assemblies of men and women who feel untouchable and to judge them as they themselves judged the world and all that goes around. I am there to come to power and not to ask it to oppose these poor which control us and which let go to their liking the companies offshore oil rigs. I am for the development of the nation. Only the interest of our federation is important and you must live for this freedom which runs in our veins and not for your personal interest.

You must forget the interest and think only of the nation and what you can make for it. Keep with you and sing to the sound of gun for this standard Viking which, by the breath of the dragon, protected, fought against the enemies of the plains of our ancestors to today. It is not any more time to collect but abolish the privileges and to destroy forever the system which directs us. I am able to only live for my grounds and I am ready with any sacrifice. One cannot give to the intellectuals the load of the nation nor that of the army and its defense. In any event, one should not be defended but attack! Yes to attack the enemies. It will come one day when the son of the dragon will take up arms and will embank the enemies until the end as thousand years ago. I do not tell you not that I do not want to see of veiled woman. We are well beyond these disputes. I do not want to see any more any foreigner at home for the moment. Time that our grounds find their fertility and, if it is necessary, to receive some from them. Then it will be under our conditions. Any person who will violate our laws will be put at death to show our determination not to turn over never again behind.

Today, I do not celebrate the 100 years of a war but the memory of these impostors who wanted that we destroy ourselves, us Gothic people Celtic Vikings, to get rid of us and this with an only aim of eliminating our races and our tribes. But it St not possible because we are chosen people. That which was shown in the illumination which generated the beginning and the end of any thing.

If we must regain our freedom inside our grounds, it should be gained. But also outside to show at which point are and to once more show we, or should I say for the last time, which we are the elite of the nations and which without us, nothing can be accomplished.

As always, we are the only ones with being able to break the Persian ones and to make them fold under our swords. Because to in no case we are not afraid of anyone to shine with the firmament of Excalibur.

I am the leader wanted to carry out our tribes to regain our grounds step by step and to burn the enemy not to have the idea never again that it could one day exist. Yes! Today it is the festival of the greatest swindle than the world knew. This famous treaty of Versailles which made us slaves from abroad in our clean grounds. Not! It is out of the question that I submit myself to a foreigner and I do not need to give you the names because know them to you.

The horde of our enemies is ready to use any pretext to destroy us and the war will be savage. You do not wait has what I give you of the medals. But if you carry the arm-band of the TIC, then everyone will know in which camp you fight and who you are not a foreigner. Those which will not carry this arm-band will be either of impostors or from abroad. We will know it because they will put forward ideas of social justice or Community policy whereas they are either of the swindlers or of the people not being able to protest the right of blood.

I will cancel the laws of the ground in the second or I will be elected. I will also cancel straight for the foreigners. We cannot pay the same taxes, to have the same rights because we defend our grounds whereas they spit us above.

Now, we must draw up ourselves, weapons with the fist, and create in each district, each city, each canton a militia which will be directed by the protocol of the TIC and which will obey only the chiefs chosen by the council of the public hello.

Our work goes directly in the economic raising of these technocrats of the policy who fight the piece of the cake on your collective hopes.

It is the same for art and culture, where all those which are selected are friends of friends of these groups or communities from abroad who use our resources and our system since 1919 for their personal end. I, a long time ago, already had fought against these degenerated by lacerating the fabrics with the fiac. But considering this does not have is enough, I will burn oneself telling them art, a bunch of refuse that same my excrement's are of better forecasts if there is comparison possible. I will prohibit any symbols of worship, except for those of our druidic traditions. I will give again with this authority true required to be.

There is future for our empire. Therefore everyone wants to destroy us. Because if we take again the power, then the wealths will be only on our premises and they know it. We will not share anything with anybody, simple return of the things as will say the other.

What?!? Will I have to justify myself in front of unspecified idiot whereas I am at home? And me I am in the right of life or of died on any being which would not obey the law of the knighthood.

I do not have any reason to justify myself before any court. And if they believed to have by trying me to put to me in prison at the United States, I indeed made fun of them of making them believe what they wanted to hear. Because they are so proud that they forget of it that in period of war, nothing is impossible and especially not to laugh at their mediocrity.

Nobody never protected our people. Not, nobody. Since tens of years a wind blew by our traditions with the bagpipe, the kilt, the bagpipe, our dances, etc, which preserved this pride which makes that we live in a single breath of the departure of our legions for the ultimate attack. I want neither of the power nor of the money. Because all this is nothing beside the regard of my people for my acts and the glance of its clans for the honor, courage and the blue blood which froze me and runs in my veins.

The entrepreneurs make promises, but today we do not need more them and we can direct our industries without this employers which derived since too long. It is nevertheless important to know that any owner who will officialize its accounts will not be continued. For the others they will have to answer their crimes against the state, like their family. They will be shown of crime against the state and criminal conspiracy for their personal enrichment. This will have as an answer a 100 years judgment firm of prison. We must with the fatherland. The fatherland does not owe us anything. We live and use all the means of our nation and we must recognize the merit and the love to him who it owes. These policies live on the fact that

247

you received only one average education and especially that of the soft food created by consumption.

We must each and everyone create a concentration of efforts for the nation and beat us hearts and hearts for this one. If not you do not have anything to on our premises make and you must leave as fast as possible without anything, because you stole us before already enough if it is not the case then we will imprison you until your end.

That request mass except for being satisfied, in the same way that she wants to know to protect herself. We are in war and we must fight. Prepare and fit your armours and fight with all the testimony of your ancestors. There will be no exception, no possibility of flashback. It is not me which want it, it is the future of our existence. That I would be there or not, there is no possibility to be raised against the destiny of people which are there since the beginning and will be until the end by the grace of Odin.

71

14 November 2013

We give means of being the nation where the world wants
to come because we have the greatest security and the most
interesting taxes. With regard to the tax, the policy of the
middle-class was the worst and it is a disaster for humanity
to see this cohesion of the power in this dead end without
end. The taxes must be taken with the source every month
on each employee or tallies. This tax must be less a maximum
of 27%. At the end of the year, you will send a card to the tax
institution which will refund you the VAT which you will have
spent by removing it from your direct tax. The VAT must be of
maximum 8.5% and the corporation taxes must be 8.5%. All this
within the framework of the people who never wanted to steal
the institutions for those which will have through companies
screens desired to set up a conspiracy against the state. They
will be seen stopping and imprisoning. All the goods will be
seized without any possibility of unspecified arrangement.

Our people cannot find themselves today obliged to share with
the enemy, with the foreigner. Any foreigner must be regarded
as such and will not be able to receive the same rights. It is
obvious that this joke must stop and that any person having
received the nationality of one of the European territories will

see it confiscating and becoming, if it is necessary, a foreign visa. The right of the ground does not exist. We acknowledge only the right of blood and all the attempts to make us change opinion are directed near the foreigners, themselves of obscure religious confessions which live in the luxury and the lust.

The question of the political reconstruction can be made only in the order of the democratic system. And which is the guaranteeing one if not America or what is called the United States for the founded good of the federation? Yes, it is finally necessary to apply the system of after war which was set up by the Marshall plan. Plan of reconstruction ready to be redefined. Because indeed, the leaders of the time in Western Europe, such as de Gaulle, developed an ultimate pretext to indicate the dangers of the Communism which was at the time the number one enemy of Western Europe and all that one called NATO.

Besides yes all this makes me so much laugh! Because today, all these people who go on the plates TVS were during after war of dangerous terrorists. And under their social pace, these leftists are lamentable extremists ready with very to destroy the founded goods of Europe which they wanted plain but which, at the time, was in the grip of a common enemy: Stalin.

Yes, that there even whose Communists and Front de Gauche do not want to evoke in spite of the most 85 million died of the concentration camps created by the KGB and not by German. These camps functioned with full mode by 1927 when any political idea other that the Stalinist Bolchevism was to be irradiated for the good of the people and their leaders.

Stalin. The enemy of American. The enemy of the people. That which was called the small father. Dangerous, gives, unstable, mentally ill... But how could we forget these elements which made this left a total drift of the right and concepts? Not of the republic but of the policies which have controls Europe during hundreds of years.

Yes this same Stalin allowed has de Gaulle to found a system where the Marshall plan could not be set up. Because the American fear made it possible to these new European leaders to have a power if the assembly and the senate would not fulfill the requirements of the president or the Prime Minister. Yes, the policy of after war lived herself between collaborationist's and communist terrorist who had hidden under the aegis of resistance. So easy to shout revenge when one can see and speak under a freedom which our army protects!

It was necessary costs that costs to prepare the handing-over in value of our states. To be ready to extend the capacity of cohesion of our people to create a resistance lends to very to predetermine our will to be the only winners. We cannot accept these idiocies of documentaries any more showing us untouchable cities oneself saying with foreign people who would make the law. It is time to make the vacuum and to sterilize any person not returning in the row, that it is one robber or a journalist. I will take again the power of an iron hand and I will not make any compromised negotiation nor. They will see that I do not joke. The armies which will dedicate allegiance with the nation will be ordered for the good even our nation. We will accept any more any dispute nor no lie. We will send in prison all these people who are not our blood and our will cancel all the rights like made Stalin before us. And the leftists will be glad to see that I take again word for word the commands of this communist policy which was worth to be the state in its power.

We will not consolidate our nation with weapons. Never with men who have the feeling and who want more than one state of straw but of a size which gives them the goose flesh when they hear the anthem of the winners.

I am decided to beat me on the victory and I will be able to die in peace when all this dirtiness is out of my ground. I do not have shame nor fear of saying what my people I think do not want to see this traveling dustbin more and I am ready to cope with all the attacks. This book is not made to like but explain my policy. I will not change. And to give to feet our nation, we must evacuate all the refuse which is here since very little time.

Today, our people are ready to fight until the victory and we will be victorious. Because you are cowards, who in any event have neither eduction nor culture. You are not used for nothing. You are nothing and your existence does not have any utility for our companies. Your parents and grandparents showed as much cowardice. They came to work without fighting to understand where was the fight of their people. To flee its country is to give up the fundamental good to create wealth and, of course, of living and dying for the action to be. Still is necessary it to have the philosophical spirit.

I do not want to hear any more of the police and the army: "it is not possible" but "YES CHIEF!" And to give on level this nomenclature. Who will follow the spirit even of my diligence without seeking another thing to live under the direction of my faith?

My movement is perhaps young in the title, but exists since always and will give again with our nations work and prosperity as it is due.

72

15 November 2013

Yesterday Communism took without concession the grounds of the peasants for the optimization of the chiefs of the party. Today, it is the socialism which took your grounds by the taxes to you. We cannot accept a company directed by the poor ones who do not know our cultures and which think of being able to destroy us under the founded good of their own interest.

It is nevertheless extremely odd to think of releasing itself from the people who came on our premises. So foolish whereas it is of our right to awake and not to more accept these lies created of any part to control us. The soldiers do not have any more any definition in our great nation and they do not know even any more in what really their role is important.

We were trotted between war and passion whereas we are plain in the same culture and we come from the same center for the same destiny. We must today raise us and impose to us. Nobody frightens us. We must finally release us from these occupants who, like formerly, oppress us and oblige us to fold us with their culture. It is unacceptable to authorize it or to allow it. We are not the symbol of a Utopian freedom but only the petrol even of the people which fought and died for generally accepted ideas of their last testimony. The democracy about which you speak does not exist. There is no word to describe it so much it is impossible to imagine for a child. And yet it is well as this which to you present it. With each time I can express myself, you offend me with insults. Because yes, you do not show your faces and only insult them come from pseudonyms of which one knows nothing.

We since the treaty of Versailles are obliged to excuse to us in front of one by ground of a nullity which does not want any for our people but indeed the desire to dig our death.

The religion cannot exist in our company because it is quite simply personal. But it is necessary to acknowledge take a religion without putting question at the 21st century the poverty of a civilization shows which continues to believe in a world which does not exist. Because there is god nor of paradise. Only and single life is low besides here and does not have the equal one. They is indeed the hooligans who are made pass to be of the monks who are largest impostors of this company.

We must thus reconquer our territories and sterilize any person who would be against. Because behind this human would hide an idea to destroy our nation. Any person being aware of what I bring as message will give an account by itself which I am there to awake these enthusiast spirits of freedom. That there even which led our people to uncover us and to leave the brooks where us had been *engeôlés*.

73

4 December 2013

It is necessary to destroy vermin politicarde in the name of the citizen. Yes we must sterilize this vermin which is propagated. It is enough to be posed in Paris to see this horror in front of us... But not only in Paris obviously. What Paris today if not the reflection of the world? A capital attacked by the foreigners as if it were a steamer boat people that believe very allowed and who do not comply with any rule. Pose you to it question. Why the foreigners come on our premises of course the answers fuse: in the answers we have the famous one of course, that of self saying freedom which as a powder of perlimpinpin is put in all sauces of all the parties and in all the discussions. But our country is especially the country of the human rights and the citizen. But that is what that wants to say if not that of this would remake has our national Robespierre to see his idea and concept besides well near of that to Lénine. Yes. The human rights are not a vulgar banner such publicity which would praise the rights of a detergent has to have enzymes but indeed rights which concede with the citizens the rights of which good citizenship. In fact, the king is not the only one to fight for the rights but each citizen must enforce laws. Let us imagine for example a car to pass to red light. And well your right is to make a photograph of this person and to send it to the website of denunciation for rape of the law. And yes I say rape well because this is one. But it is not only that and I do not want to minimize the rights and the work of each one. The civil rights are those to work for the good of the nation and not of another nation. Indeed if you decide to live in France for example then you must forget your country of origin. If not why are you here? And in this case fight on your territory what will be much more honorable besides of your share. Attention the lie is prohibited on our premises. Stop taking the banner of the rights for your personal rights.

Yes, you do not have any right. But you have only duties. The first: to respect the order.

It is necessary to stop saying anything in particular on the subject to be French: to be French is to be heir to the Frank people.

Yes, being French it is a being a franc. But what is a franc? For uncultivated not it is not a Swiss coin but people known as Aryan comprising tribes, clans and families. I.e. a whole well defined hierarchy. As you see it, frank being is not close to everyone. To be French, this right to carry the crowns of our ancestors and not with a vulgar piece of paper given by collaborationist's who have of cease only to disparage our company to take it out of clipper and finally to have it. I will refer so that it occurred to Cracow and to this admirable king Casimir the Large who wanted to be open for the foreign people which would come in his capital to share happiness to be free under the laws that it had developed and during 7 centuries. These foreigners for the majority plundered in their personal interest.

Yes to be frank is to be French, German, Polish, Italian, Spanish, Hungarian, etc

Here a definition of the Frank word, drawn from several

encyclopedias:

> *"frankly (Latinized enfrancus) the free man will indicate,*
> *but it is only by one shift in posterior meaning, an adjective*
> *drawn from the proper name. The radical is the old man*
> *norroisfrakka, which would suppose that the franque league*
> *would have drawn its name from a totemic weapon. The*
> *forms old man norroisfrekkr "bold, courageous, intrepid,*
> *valiant".*

The frank people are before a whole people of warriors who elected and placed themselves freely for the military business under the authority of a war leader appointed by the princes called jarl, named rex francorum, "king of the Francs", which exerted their authority in their gawi (cf néerl. gouw, all. Gau), or pagus "administrative canton".

I now will be much more expansive and I know how the pseudonyms journalists hidden in their seat well soft will have either the word to repeat something or to criticize me out of fear of seeing itself excommunicating our territories forever. By that, I will take the metaphor of a hospital to speak about the sterilization of this one and need to apply it to our nation.

Yes it is necessary for us to sterilize because it is impossible to set out again on bases which they same were rotted by vermin. Let us imagine a rotted tree and a policy who knows there nothing and which would come to tell you that you can do it, to set out again. You know very well that it is necessary to cut the stock to hope that the sap, blood of this mineral, takes again life. It is the same with the state (branches) which not only rotted, but also the trunk which is reached. It is necessary to cut all that it represents to set out again on the bases which will make us to it chosen people. That which will be able to find its power, its honor and its courage.

Our middle-class is rotted to marrow. It is lamentable to cling to vulgar privileges which make of it the worst enemy of the state nation. It should be sterilized and it is incredible that the chief of a structure can make return its family like a declining nobility bourbonnaise and Napoleonean. Only the work given to the state nation must be encouraged and glorified by prices given to the people to show the descent lends to still prove and still its to provide and its position of leader. After my death, much among you who will have approached me and been pleased to share moments of life with me will say that I was extremely intelligent. And it is well for this reason that I find myself in front of you. Not only because I am the heir, but because in me you find the values of your forefathers.

Serious resistance cannot be made on behalf of this middle-class which was let take in a kind of weakness which took them has part of a state, government of robbers, and which would have of their giving wings to fight against impostors and to come to us since long time.

The middle-class was blind and was let plug because happy to benefit from a system which she believed to dominate, of which she was only tenant and by this fact which gave him the power to say not to the private banking debt. But we will reconsider this subject before the end of volume 1.

The lie was the chief of these years to believe in a Marshall plan which was dedicated to the failure because he answered directly the destruction of the European markets and the control of those by the American state, increasingly larger and more envious to destroy Europe, because only rampart with this policy of the Middle-East. These technocrats of the congress and the senate eager to benefit for the families owners from the EDF bank.

No attempts economic was considered by the governments of 1948 has today. Because the only goal of Europe was on the one hand to create an anti Stalinist sovietism and on the other hand anti Russo-poutinisme. All that with an aim of serving Big Brother.

You speak to defend of the vital economic credits and yet you are not ready to sacrifice you and especially to beat you for this passion which is the only one for which should have a little regard to you. Stop looking at what you can gain and think only of the State nation for the pleasure of being and of being part of this family which is our people: Francs.

Yes one needs honor to make party of our people, one needs illegal blood and not papers which give you the single right to make you forget. But it is what you did not understand and that we will render comprehensible to you by taking again all until you disappear - finally from our world - and which you join your childish beliefs of a world of beyond which does not exist. You are only children without utility who do not deserve to see and to feel the lights of the life.

You are not even any more of the skilled workers but of impostors come to steal our goods and to completely bathe us with remarks mild nutters and quite irrational in this 21st century which still sounds in your head like that of 7th.

The public goods do not belong to you and you must regard them as goods which are called after a chance that others do not have because they are not supplied as we are it. Your selfishness is the proof of non the direction and which you do not have anything to make in this fight against the systems which made you people oneself saying legal whereas you are only enemies of the state nation. And we will make you pay all the evil which you made with your own goods.

74

15 November 2013

The displacement of the suburbs of the CzechRepublic in Pantin. I was invited to Prague and in Moravie, passing by the Bohemian one to discover there a landscape in charge of images of the unhappy past of this Stalinism which, like a bulldozer, had crushed any attempt to think differently. The landscapes were always same the, in charge ones of Soviet stories and I put to think of this wretched image of these are worth anything which not only destroyed our suburbs for one does not know which reason, but moreover complained not to have better. Yes, this show in Czech republic of these Marxist Russo buildings the ones against the others had not changed and most people of the east continued to live as those without complaining but especially by making all their possible to preserve the little which they had. Yes, these cities quite worse than ours were however like works of art, liked these beings which continued to want to save their little of dignity, contrary to our foreigners the purpose of who were only to only destroy. As the governments will not do anything then I will take again in hand all this system to change it forever and especially not to more see the images which whip televisions on our premises showing people of refuse living.

We must gain our freedom inside and outside. We must give again with the army a dignity to intervene in all the cases and of living under a domination of common property. The increasingly many tourists to see the hours of glory passed through our people must be astonished by this ground which will enlarge our capacity to give the benefit of our economy and the leader of the new capitalization.

Displacement in Europe enabled me to see and understand at which point we had been fooled and used. The people of the east asked me why we had as many foreigners whereas the journalists representing vermin in France did not have that the word with the mouth of percentage which oneself saying was to be an index surely created of any parts by themselves. I could only answer and felt me constrained knowing that they were right. Yes, all these foreigners who came to steal the bread of my children and who in more did not hesitate to spit me above. I was happy of this book which I wrote by telling me that finally, if I died, this book would be the guideline of the future generations and that they would come to fight to save our Europe. While becoming prisoner with the United States, I understood that the whole world was racist, and much more than us.

That the religions were only one given political force to bring a man and one man to the power. I discovered groups which astonished me because they did not have to in no case lost their faith to be of this continent of Europe and to be Aryan race. Word which had been excluded from my vocabulary because attached to one completed time of a last war which had used almost all the symbols Vikings, Celtic, Gothic and by people who were not even our tribes. Then why? All these questions which resounded in my head since adolescence and this oneself saying problem which was not one but which had been created by this wretched conspiracy of these intruders set up to destroy my people.

Then, leaning me in prison on these tribes ready with all but which had forgotten that their fight was in Europe and not in the United States. Even if America had been at one time the place of the desires of world creation in a small island of freedom for tribes from Europe which had suffered already from the lie and impostors.

75

7 December 2013

The policy, networks, the debt and the banking system.

The policies for whom you vote do not know any more than you.

Then you will tell me: "yes but they have technocrats who can lay the solutions to them". But in this case, how to continue a political program without competence? Isn't this the same thing as to want to raise cattle without anything not to know there? It is in any event a new heresy and the policies must be single people, ready with very to defend the right of the State nation and wanting to live and fight for a flag which floats well high by its size and its frankness.

The problems of contacts and connection are much larger when one knows that it is necessary before to be in agreement with, not only the adjoining countries, but with the groups which form the economy of oil has the Internet. The policies arrive at stations without having any contact in the worlds policy, economic or even financier. Considering they never traveled and do not know to in no case the chiefs of tribes of State, etc For example, in Saudi Arabia, protocol prohibited the princes from speaking to the men who are not same row and who are not Moslem. Thus either you are able to trace your genetic heritage or you have the proof of your "muslumanity". And still is necessary it to be of a tribe which conceives the wahibism and not the poor of the Maghreb which are taken, by the modes of the Middle-East, like underdeveloped slaves.

Indeed, it is through the travel and my meetings, very young person, by my grandfather, that I could meet and see how the other countries lived. And I was of course scandalized when the people in Europe spoke about racism whereas all these continents lived it in a completely honorable way. Often the questions fused near my grandfather. Why accept such and such people in your schools? And my grandfather unceasingly repeated that was to develop spirits which could change their own economic vision and policy necessary for a near future. The emirs, often grumbled, and declared themselves completely against the idea that a woman could go in a school, as well as a man of a lower caste. I listened and threw invades of a feeling of hatred and war. Gradually I understood that these African, Asian chiefs wanted only their own interest whereas I had grown in the spirit to be a great nation through the Vikings people which generate the vitality and the spirit of all our cause.

I had understood nevertheless how the networks were important. Since the 7 years age, I built my address book from Los Angeles to Shanghai, of Entertainment to the policy. Without the knowledge I developed strategies which one day would not only be used for to me to defend but also to tackle the desired moment.

Very young person, I got information about the debt and qualities of an economy which had known to exploit the interest against the Stalinism which had lost its reason to give states of an extreme poverty which one saw the pillars not supporting more the system with the fall of the Berlin Wall. Yes but then which system was good? That to be made plunder by a political regime in the name of one only man or by impostors creating a group of a pseudonym intelligentsia being distributed the world treasure under the work of the blue-collar workers? In both cases the system went to the explosion because in any case there was not a genuine machine lends to establish a neutrality.

The system had since the second world war taken of the aspects of secret society where converted Jews wanted to be the noble ones, at the point to accept any lowness of it and while rewriting history. And yes. In only one click they had succeeded in creating laws for themselves, such as that 1973 called law Pompidou or law Rothschild. How to provide to accept this law and why did nobody change it so far? Which are lownesses of this secret society to have still the power? I will be able well - sure to explain these laws but the problem is that it is not only and that today all Europe answers these loans of state of the private banks where your taxes are used for paying the interest and enriching about ten families which do not want any to share though it is with you. And when a man as me arrives and that they see that I can come to power, they try to threaten me to make me kill, to throw me in prison to make me disappear forever. Yes but here. They had forgotten a note with their symphony and I left all their conspiracies.

I realized very very young person that the mission of the State nation was to réétablir the concept of the knighthood.

However, my desire is not to defend a kind of system platonien but indeed to defend this nation Gothic Celtic Viking which is formed by this Europe which goes from the ocean to the steppes of Russia. Our tribes must all give to achieve this spot and to destroy the enemy to overcome and consolidate this dreamed who, since the caves of Lascaux, places us as a cradle of humanity.

I am not there to make like each and everyone of the populism history recover voices at the minorities and make them believe in my devotion. Not, I am there to begin again costs whom our empire costs and I am ready to die for this cause which, from this fact, should be only and single opportunity of living in this ocean of unhappiness and declines where all our values more than were ridiculed and indeed forgotten at the point to more know what we are.

I do not need to invent me or create a history. We are the history! And the will to be is in front of us. We must now be the police of the state nation and so in the past we established the famous committees then give them to judge all that will leave our rights and our duties.

76

9 December 2013

Victory of our action and the return of our company leader of the worldwide market.

Incapacity to solve the problems. You all are leaning about the extremes or the middles called centrists or other mobilities whereas you seek a chief. Because too many vermins appear while trying to carry out groups which could give an opinion. Still one needs a truth and still better a cause to generate the immortality of a movement.

I speak to you to adhere to a party which represents officially all that you are and who gives you all that you wish to share. I do not propose to you to belong to a movement but of a family where all we will be a link to give in our state nation a new image. Do not forget which we are, even if you received all since the second world war a new definition of the History. You know, at the bottom of you, that something does not turn out badly and does not correspond to the values which formerly carried you by these grandparents who represented one moment of freedom and joy.

Our menhirs and our druids are as many chances as to be able to go up on this virgin throne which expects since such

an amount of time this combative knight who, being afraid of
nothing, wanted to see in you this exceptional destiny of honor
and courage.

The comedy lasted enough and it is time to put an end at it.
We must take again the weapons and put all to us in row for
the European order. This federation of the areas where all our
cultures, our languages and our traditions will be respected and
heard. But still to much more give again with our areas this local
color than everyone envies us.

I do not have anything against the foreigner, since he is the
foreigner. The moment of the kindness Viking disappeared
well and I do not want to make any concession any more. It is
necessary to take again all the assets and all the goods of these
impostors and to condemn them to perpetuity in prisons where
only the bread and water will be granted to them, without more
any possibility of communicating with outside.

It came the moment when the prophecy of Nostradamus must
be carried out. This prince of north will raise his weapons of
the east to the west. He will reconquer been in hiding after
the other by giving again with each one his existence and will
protect forever this empire which will remain until the end of
the worlds.

It came the moment to hear that the second world war was
only the release of the third war and that the merchants believed
to gain still this war then which will be the total destruction
their agreements made with generals impaled on the public
places.

All your existence, and even today, you saw grotesque policies
and journalists to give you a significance of the world, of their
world has them, in middle-class apartments with for ultimate
desire the disproportionate gentrification. We have in front of

us enemies and we must get rid some costs whom costs. All the armed fractions representing Europe which were even exiled will return to take again our ground fatherland together. This ground which, in my hand, has the black color and will be soon red of blood to destroy the malignant one and to save the fruit of the peasant who, all its life worked hard to see rising this strong and useful tree.

The enemies are against us since 1945 out of fear of seeing our true empire redrawing itself without them. And they are right. To in no case we do not need them. When I think of all these leaders coming from my family who could give so much freedoms to people unable to thank and which we arrived at ultimate confrontation. Yes, the outcome is present and you all must beat you with our with dimensions to defend the values of yesteryear against the enemy who declared himself.

Do not forget how you can follow the party and what you can give him to gather you under a military behavior and an emblem which floats and flaps to the sound of bugle. If the concept to be is difficult to define in practice, the differences of the clans give us the possibility of rejoining us with the same blood to fight in the same vein.

The solidarity of each individual preserves the care to determine in the belief, the direction of only one will. It is scandalous to see how much people walk today the "racist" word on their faces, and how much people have a false personal design of this concept all while adapting it to a completed system which wants to be believed immoral. Racism wants nothing to say. It is simply the reflection of politicians much more wormy than one wants to claim it, hiding through words which make oneself saying horror. This call without end of the second world war and its horrors is only one denunciation campaign, a manner of believing in an assumption well not very possible. And in any event, did one see a war of Napoleon in the love and the intoxication of the feelings which the man could have had for the next? All the religious doctrines wanted to make accept the man who it was more intelligent than the animal, therefore less malicious, which is absolutely not true. How can one leave in life people who steal the every day and are not condemned? Time came so that the truth is made and to denounce all impostors, to seize their goods and to destroy the families forever so that never nobody can return.

Our victory, it is a determining point of a militant policy where each one wants to give to our fatherland at the cost of its blood. And I will be the first to do it. To redraw on my flesh the symbol of our adhesion to the breath of the dragon.

We are once again in search of Graal for finally living in peace in our obedience within our territories. A ground, a chief, a law.

We are already victorious because they are afraid of us. They know that I will not do any the concessions that the others made before me. There will be no pity nor of compassion for these dogs of sold which wanted our loss. The courts of the public committee will go to full mode. We will release for the last time this time of malignant our world which will see the reflection of intoxication to be ourselves: the Vikings, Celtic, Gothic people.

References

Kingdom of Normandy
www.kingdomofnormandy.com

Kingdom of Nova Francia
www.novafrancia.com

Liberté-Nation Project
www.liberte-nation.com

www.ingramcontent.com/pod-product-compliance
Lightning Source LLC
Chambersburg PA
CBHW062203270326
41930CB00009B/1630